Advance Praise
Moving to Mexico's Lake Chapala

"I found it highly readable, most comprehensive, and flawlessly organized. I think it's the best book of its kind that I have read, and I have been down here for 25 years."
    Alejandro Grattan-Dominguez
    Editor-in-Chief, El Ojo del Lago Magazine

"I've lived at Lakeside for ten years now, and coordinate the Information Desk at the Lake Chapala Society. Yet I'm amazed at how much I learned reading this book. I fully intend to keep a copy at the Information Desk, and suggest all the volunteers familiarize themselves with it."
    Harriet Hart
    Lakeside writer

"I thoroughly enjoyed the read. I wish I had your book available when I moved here 8 years ago. It certainly would have made life simpler and more interesting."
    Howard Feldstein
    President, Lake Chapala Society

"A valuable resource for anyone visiting or moving to Lake Chapala. If you can, buy it before you come. At the very least, buy it the moment you arrive. Having this book when I moved here 11 years ago would have saved me many missteps and countless hours of research."
    Judy Dykstra-Brown
    Lakeside writer and artist

Moving to Mexico's Lake Chapala

Checklists, How-To's, and
Practical Information and Advice
for Expats and Retirees

First Edition

Lisa L. Jorgensen
Mexico Expat Press
Ajijic, Jalisco, Mexico

www.MovingToMexicosLakeChapala.com
Jorgensen@MovingToMexicosLakeChapala.com

First Edition

Copyright © 2012 by Lisa L. Jorgensen

All international rights reserved. No part of this book may be reproduced in any form by any means, electrical or mechanical, including photocopying, recording, storing in any information retrieval system, or transmitting without prior written permission from the copyright holder. Reviewers may quote brief extracts in a review.

The information presented in this guide is the most current as of the published date. It is not intended to replace legal or medical professionals' counsel. The publisher and author disclaim any liability to any party for any loss or damage caused by errors, omissions, or any disruption of plans, events, or outcomes.

Neither the author nor the publisher receives any personal, commercial, or financial consideration from any merchants or services presented herein.

ISBN 978-0-9859476-0-6

Mexico Expat Press
PMB 71-3066
Carretera Oriente #54 Interior
45920 Ajijic, Jalisco, Mexico

For additional copies, visit:
www.MovingToMexicosLakeChapala.com, or
www.Amazon.com, or
booksellers and gift stores in the Lake Chapala area.

To submit corrections/additions to the next edition, email: Jorgensen@MovingToMexicosLakeChapala.com

Contents

Forward 9

Introduction 13

Part 1
Your Exploratory Trip 17
    Chapter 1
    Planning Your Trip 18
    Chapter 2
    During Your Trip 24

Part 2
Before Your Move 37
    Chapter 1
    Consider Your Finances 38
    Chapter 2
    Choosing Your Move Date 41
    Chapter 3
    Telling Your Family and Friends 42
    Chapter 4
    What About Your Pets? 44
    Chapter 5
    What To Do About Your House 47
    Chapter 6
    What About Your Car? 50
    Chapter 7
    What About Your Other Belongings? 52
    Chapter 8
    Four Weeks Before Moving 64
    Chapter 9
    Three Weeks Before Moving 71
    Chapter 10
    Two Weeks Before Moving 77
    Chapter 11
    One Week Before Moving 81

Part 3
Your Move 85
> *Chapter 1*
> Driving to the Border 86
> *Chapter 2*
> At the Mexican Border..90
> *Chapter 3*
> Driving to Lake Chapala 96

Part 4
Your First Month at Lake Chapala 99
> *Chapter 1*
> Your First Week..100
> *Chapter 2*
> Your Second Week 110
> *Chapter 3*
> Your Third Week 112
> *Chapter 4*
> Your Fourth *Week*..114

Part 5
Living at Lake Chapala 117
> *Chapter 1*
> Legal Basics 120
> *Chapter 2*
> The Towns 123
> *Chapter 3*
> Language and Social Customs 132
> *Chapter 4*
> Getting Around 143
> *Chapter 5*
> Shopping 163
> *Chapter 6*
> Safety 187

Part 5 (continued)
Living at Lake Chapala

Chapter 7
Medical Care 190
Chapter 8
Home Life and Services 202
Chapter 9
Utilities 214
Chapter 10
Technology 219
Chapter 11
Banking 231
Chapter 12
Government Services 236

Appendix 249

Exploratory Trip Checklist 249
Move Planning Checklist 250
Border Checklist 253
Moving In Checklist 254
Emergency Numbers and Words 256
Telephone Dialing 259
Web Boards, Forums, and Blogs 261
Recommended Reading 262
Places and Services 264
Jalisco Driving Laws and Fines 266
Federal Driving Laws and Fines 282
Vehicle Accident Form 290
Common Conversions 299

Index 301

Acknowledgements

For their kind contributions, support, and advice, my sincerest thanks to Karen Blue, Francine Britton, Alejandro Grattan-Dominguez, Kim Jorgensen, Spencer McMullen, Rosemary Dineen, Harriet Hart, Howard Feldstein, Terry Vidal, and Judy Dykstra-Brown.

Forward

I read through "Moving to Mexico's Lake Chapala" just as I was approaching my sixth month of living in Ajijic, Mexico as a newly minted semi-retiree, and knew for sure that Lisa Jorgensen had "been there and done that" on every single page.

Lisa Jorgensen has created the ultimate resource for anyone thinking of, dreaming about, or actually planning to move to the Lake Chapala area. Her solid research, fact-finding, trial and error problem solving, and persistence in finding the correct answers to questions, the right directions to places, and the names of various people to contact and talk to, is very timely, as well as time-saving and relevant.

Most books pertaining to the Lake Chapala region of Mexico were written at least five, and up to ten years ago. Income requirements, laws, and safety issues needed to be re-researched, updated, and written about. Lisa Jorgensen has so very kindly done this.

Especially helpful is the process that takes the reader from entering the country on a tourist card to acquiring residency status, with answers to the "who, what, when, where, and how" of each process.

Lisa's voice of reason in being able to separate fact from fiction and rumors from truths will be useful in the decision making process, whether the person reading this book plans to retire, semi-retire, or commute back and forth to the US or Canada on a seasonal basis every six months or so.

Lisa's presentation style, mixed with anecdotal information, wit, and humor takes the book into the realm of pleasure reading. Her perceptions as she integrates into full-time living in the Lake Chapala area are insightful, grounded in reality, and give the reader a tremendous fund of knowledge. Once a decision to move to the Lake Chapala area is made by the reader, the to-do lists simply help things fall into place as each item is checked off.

Once the reader's move is completed, and he or she is living in the area, Lisa offers logical advice, further to-do lists, and guidelines for the first few weeks of entry into a brand new life.

Practical information about foreign customs, etiquette, culture, and the day-to-day way of life in Mexico are also covered. Lisa also provides relevant information on learning the Spanish language, how extensive this should be or not be, and advice and correct protocol to use with housekeepers, gardeners, staff in restaurants, grocery stores, and even the beauty salon. Lisa talks about local customs, the economy, and gives an overview of current local, state, and national politics.

Forward

She kindly gives readers information on driving in Mexico. Especially helpful are the forms in the back of the book on what to do in case of an auto accident, and the clear-cut, no-nonsense information that an accident is considered a "crime" in Mexico, and how the laws are very different from the US and Canada.

This book will surely become the authoritative guide on coping with the challenges, as well as the joys, of living in the Lake Chapala region of Mexico.

My only regret in reading the book is that I did not have it in hand to read before I moved to Ajijic in March of 2012. Needless to say, having this book would have saved me hours of time, days of decreased anxiety, and many months of scattered research trying to figure out how to do this move completely on my own with mostly outdated information.

That being said: I left the small town of Lenox, Massachusetts on March 1, 2012 in a brand new car packed with meager but meaningful possessions, a GPS, a few maps, and good written directions. I drove 3,400 miles through the US, crossed the border at Laredo, Texas, and allowed myself two days to get to Lake Chapala. I got that wonderful green light we all dream of, survived one military checkpoint and car search, one police checkpoint, and arrived in Ajijic to start the latest chapter of my life on March 9, 2012. Yes, I was terrified one minute, exhilarated and excited the next (I had not driven for 26 years, and had just obtained a new five-year driver's license. The trip went really well, and the drive through the breath-taking Sierra Madres was the experience of a lifetime.

Meeting Lisa, getting to know her these past few months, and hearing about the book as it progressed has been a true joy. Her thorough research, on-the-ground interviews, and persistence will benefit us all. Lisa Jorgensen's book is a definite "must read" for those who plan to live in this amazing part of Mexico, or who are already living here. Enjoy! I surely did (and if anyone could teach me to parallel park – I'd be grateful).

Francine Britton
August 2012
Ajijic, Jalisco, Mexico

Note: Francine Britton is the author of six books published by Hodder/Stoughton in London, and is writing a memoir of what it was like to live and work in twenty-nine countries. She now lives happily in Ajijic, Jalisco, Mexico.

Introduction

I've been watching the avocado dangling over my head as I write in my back yard. Having only seen avocados in supermarkets in the US, I didn't know how long this one would take to ripen – whether it would be ready before this book was. But it has kept up with me quite well, rounding out at about the same rate as this book.

A year ago, I could not have imagined that I would be sitting under an avocado tree in Mexico, living this new life. After building a full corporate career in the US, and spending a few years owning and operating an international online retail business on the East Coast, I decided the time had come for me to retire. I was burned out on 7-day-a-week, 10-hour days on the computer, and I was barely making a profit during the recession. My quality of life was flat, and I was in a rut. In other words, I needed to find a new way to live. After making a list of my priorities and criteria, I spent some time doing research on the internet, looking for the best places in the world to retire comfortably on my Social Security retirement benefits. That place turned out to be the Lake Chapala area in the state of Jalisco in Mexico.

Life for me has become a wonder, one that I would wish upon you, too, if you're ready. You don't have to be ready to retire, necessarily. You just have to be ready for a richer life. Many other people have already decided that they were ready, with over 7,000 expats (up to 15,000 in the winter) now living in the Lake Chapala area. And, many retirement guides are claiming that Lake Chapala is better than Florida for retiring baby boomers because it's less expensive (you can live well on $1,200 per month per person here), it's less humid, it's culturally rich, and the health care is excellent. Most of us are from the US and Canada. Some have come as "snowbirds", escaping cold weather in winter. Others have come as "sunbirds", escaping hot and humid weather in summer. And some, like me, have come as "lifebirds" – here to stay.

What do we do all day? The expatriate community is quite social. Some play bridge several times a week, some go to the hot springs, some play golf on beautiful green courses, some volunteer at animal shelters. Some go to the library, and meet people in the parks and plazas. We even have theater groups to get involved in. But, of course, you can do those things north of the border, too. What we really do is experience life differently.

We go to the bustling open markets in the same way that our Mexican neighbors have for hundreds of years. We watch *folklórico* dancers spin and smile in their vivid striped skirts, just as they've also done for hundreds of years. Guadalajara, Mexico's second largest city, is less than an hour away, with its shopping, museums and culture, magnificent colonial architecture, nightlife, and sophistication. We watch children dance to the local mariachi bands their fathers play in. We learn their

Introduction

language and their customs, and get included in their large extended families. We get to experience a slower, more thoughtful pace of living (and cooking). Our minds free up so we can explore our artistic or literary sides. And, we get to experience the warm and generous natures of the Mexican people, in a land full of surprises and deep beauty, in one of the best climates in the world.

I moved from the US to Lake Chapala in early 2012 with two dogs, two cats, and an SUV. This book was conceived during that trip out of my own need for information and advice. As most people do when they consider moving to a new country, I read the travel books about the region, as well as blogs and forums. But it became apparent that some important information was missing: advice on how to accomplish the move, and then practical knowledge of everyday living in this area, especially the sort of information I needed in the first month. For instance, I had questions about:

- Language – can I get along without knowing more Spanish than "Mi casa es su casa"? (Answer: yes)
- Driving – Should I take my car, or buy one there?
- Laws – Innocent until proven guilty? (Answer: not necessarily.)
- Safety – Isn't it dangerous there? (Answer: no)
- Health and insurance – What options do I have? What about Medicare?
- Food and water – What's safe to eat and drink, and what isn't?

What I really needed was a helpful neighbor who knew how to plan for the move, and who knew the ins and outs of living here. So, that's how I hope you will come to think of this book – as a friendly neighbor close at hand with lots of useful information. The purpose is definitely not to ruin your joy of discovering things for yourself. You'll notice that there are no recommendations for restaurants, bed-and-breakfast hotels, hot spring spas, or points of interest. I leave that to the travel books, and to your own explorations and adventures.

Rather, while planning your move, and during the first few months when many important decisions need to be made, this practical day-to-day living guide is here to save you time, headaches, stomach aches, money – and even a night in the pokey for both you and your car.

The avocado over my head is ripe now, but I've also been watching a small bunch of green bananas lately, growing in the far corner of my yard. Life grows so abundantly here, even in the smallest of ways.

Lisa L. Jorgensen
Ajijic, Jalisco, Mexico
August 2012

Part 1

Your Exploratory Trip

The best way to discover for yourself whether this life is right for you is to come to Lake Chapala for an exploratory trip. It will really be a vacation, but with a purpose: to determine whether the Lake Chapala area could be right for you for the long term. The time of year you choose doesn't really matter. It's always beautiful.

But you will want to plan carefully so you'll get the most out of your stay, which the following chapters, together with the Exploratory Trip Checklist in the Appendix, will help you do most effectively.

Chapter 1

Planning Your Trip

The first step is for you to know what your needs and wants are, and to make a list of them. Do you need top quality schools for your children? Do you want to be in an area with arts and theatre? Do you want to be in an area with lots of other expats, or would you rather live in a more integrated way with traditional Mexican neighbors? How important are each of the criteria you choose? At the end of your trip, you can use your list to decide whether the Lake Chapala area will meet your needs, and which neighborhoods you'd like best. Put your concerns on your list, too. The list will end up being highly personal to you, of course, but I can tell you that for me, the three biggest concerns were:

1. Can I live reasonably well on my US Social Security retirement benefits alone? The answer was yes. A minimum of $1,200 per month for a single, or $1,600 for a couple is enough for a decent living in this area. This amount can come from some combination of dividends, interest, retirement, and social security benefits, or you can continue earning money through an internet or consulting business -- one that doesn't require you to be present in your home country very often. You can scrape by on less than that amount, if you really need to (most Mexicans do, after all), but you may not be eligible

Your Exploratory Trip: Planning Your Trip

for an FM-3 visa, which means that you will have to cross the border and re-enter Mexico every 6 months with your car (if you have one). Please see the Index for more information about visas.

2. Will the quality and cost of health care meet my needs? The answer was yes. The quality of health care at Lakeside is very good, and in Guadalajara, less than an hour away, health care is world class. My Mexican private health care insurance costs $242 per month compared to the $750 per month I was paying in the US for approximately the same coverage and benefits.

3. Is it reasonably safe, even for a single woman? The answer, again, was yes. The narcotics cartels are not particularly interested in expat enclaves, and the Mexican government is very interested in protecting tourist and expat communities that pour millions of dollars into their economy without taking Mexican jobs. Non-drug-related crimes do exist, but they're reasonably low in number based on the size of the area, and they involve property crime more than injury.

Many people who choose to live here do so after having been here on vacation, or after getting tired of going back and forth year after year from their native country as snowbirds or sunbirds. But for those who've never been here, taking an exploratory trip (5 days or so) to the area is a very wise step, even if, like me, you're fairly certain it's going to be the right place for you. One reason is that it will help you solidify your decision. The second reason is that your move will be easier if you have a home to go to.

If you're planning to buy a home, there are many online resources to show you which homes are available, and how much they cost. Simply Google "Chapala real estate". But you will also want to see what the different towns and neighborhoods are like in person. Your exploratory trip will be necessary for that. For some basic guidelines on the various towns, see the Index under Towns.

Incidentally, you will also see online that various tour packages are offered for prospective expats and retirees by some organizations. Be sure to research them carefully. Some are actually real estate groups that will monopolize your time while you are here, showing you only their houses for sale, and making it difficult for you to make appointments with other real estate agencies. I have talked with several people here who have had this complaint – and also that the tours seemed too expensive for what they were – captive sales tours. However, it may well be that all tours are not of this type.

If you decide not to take a package tour, and it certainly isn't necessary, make note of two or three of the most prominent real estate agencies in this area from the internet, and make an appointment with them (for different days) to show you around when you're here. There is a Multiple Listing Service here at www.chapalamls.com, so you need not feel that you'll miss any properties by not having

Your Exploratory Trip: Planning Your Trip

multiple agents. They all know about, and can show you, each others' house listings. Telephoning is the best way to reach the agencies. Even though they may have an email address, don't count on a quick email response. Also, keep in mind that Mexico's time zone corresponds to the US's Central Time, and that the country code for telephoning is 52. Mexico switches between Daylight Saving Time and Standard Time, but not necessarily on the same days as the US.

"There is a Multiple Listing Service here at www.chapalamls.com, so you need not feel that you'll miss any properties by not having multiple agents."

Until recently, all real estate was sold on a cash basis. There are now some financing options available, but they do not have as favorable rates as in the US or other countries, and the down payments are much larger. So, do ask your prospective real estate agencies about their financing options, if that is an important consideration for you.

You'll want to make sure you have a valid passport. Then, book a flight to the Guadalajara airport. By the way, as you start to imagine a life in Mexico at this point, you may be tempted, as I was, to buy the Rosetta Stone language course "Latin American Spanish" on CDs. It's an excellent course, and costs hundreds of dollars north of the border. Many border airports sell them at kiosks. But don't buy the course there. I'll tell you in a later section of this book (look up *Tianguis* in the Index) how to get the full course for about $30 USD.

The best place to stay during your visit is at one of the many good bed and breakfast hotels (B & Bs) in the area. Just Google "Lake Chapala bed and breakfast". The reason B & Bs are ideal for your first trip is that you'll have ample opportunities to talk with the owners, who know the area well. They can help you in many ways: making suggestions, pointing you in the right direction, giving you important contact names, and answering many of your specific questions. You'll probably be meeting others just like yourself over breakfast, too, with whom you can compare notes, and go out to dinner.

> *"I highly recommend staying in the town of Ajijic for your first trip, since it's a central area, and since many of the real estate and rental agencies are located there."*

I highly recommend staying in the town of Ajijic for your first trip, since it's a central area, and since many of the real estate and rental agencies are located there. When making your reservation, you'll want to ask for a first floor room if stairs are challenging for you. Also inquire about the noise in the area (roosters and night clubs).

You'll also want to ask whether they can reserve an enclosed overnight parking space for you if you plan to rent a car while you're here. On my exploratory trip, I rented a car for two of the days. I wanted to break free of my agency escorts in order to get a flavor of other neighborhoods in the area, and to visit stores and some areas of interest. You won't need to make a decision about a rental car until you get here, though. Your days will be fluid. But when you do, be sure to read the section in this book regarding Rental Cars (check the Index).

And, don't forget to bring along the Exploratory Trip Checklist located in the Appendix.

Chapter 2
During Your Trip

Once you're at the Guadalajara Airport, it's not a good idea to just rent a car and drive to Lake Chapala by yourself on your first visit to the area. Unless you speak fluent Spanish, making sense of the signs to get out of the airport and onto the right highways and beyond would be too difficult. Either take a taxi from the airport, or ask your bed and breakfast (B & B) staff if they have a driver they can recommend who can pick you up at the airport and take you directly to the B & B. The trip will take about 30 to 45 minutes to Lake Chapala, and it will cost the equivalent of about $35 USD, plus you'll want to give the driver a 10% tip.

You'll need to pay for everything in pesos, which you can get at the best exchange rate at an airport ATM machine. The way to get a taxi at the airport, if you choose to do that, is to pay at the airport taxi counter, and then take your receipt outside to the *sitio* taxi stand. *Sitio* taxi drivers are licensed, registered, and insured, and are quite trustworthy. If you do take an airport taxi, ask your B&B to email you directions in English and Spanish, which you can give to the driver.

Your Exploratory Trip: During Your Trip

When you're here at Lake Chapala, you should have two base camps: the B & B where you're staying, and the (non-profit) Lake Chapala Society, which will most likely become like a second home to you. It's located at 16 de Septiembre #16-A, right in Ajijic between Corona (also called M. Castellanos) and Bravo (also called Galeana) streets. Aside from having beautiful grounds that will soothe your spirit, there's a whole world of information, activities, classes, community postings, health screenings, volunteer and charity opportunities, and expats like yourself there. You'll want to become a member to take advantage of everything they offer. The largest Mexican library of books in English is there, which, to me, is reason enough to join. So, unless you have appointments on your first day in this area, the Lake Chapala Society should be your first stop. Here's their website: www.lakechapalasociety.com. Their offices are open from 10am to 2pm, Monday through Saturday, but the grounds are open from 9 to 5.

"You'll need to pay for everything in pesos, which you can get at the best exchange rate at any ATM machine."

Once you're there, the first thing you'll want to do is buy a map or two of the Lake Chapala area at their bookstore. The one I highly recommend is the fold-out one by Sombrero Books (cartography by Tony Burton). Another one is the Mexico Travelers Map Guide to Lake Chapala,

Ajijic and Environs by Mexico Travelers Information. I always have one in my purse and one in my car's glove compartment.

The real estate agents you've contacted will be very happy to show you the various neighborhoods and houses (be sure to take your map along, and make notes of what's where). This will be a good time for you to interview your agents, too, since real estate agents in Mexico are not formally licensed or regulated. Anyone with the proper visa or citizenship can call him/herself a real estate agent. And, they are not obligated to tell you of any defects or other issues regarding properties. For instance, some old houses have pipes that are not wide enough to allow toilet paper to pass. Either you will have to be content with using a trash container for all your used toilet paper, or you will be faced with a significant cost for upgrading the plumbing.

> *"Renting, at least for the first six months or so, may be your best option."*

There are some realty organizations that brokers and agents can join in order to enhance their credibility, but these are not true licensing agencies. The local organization is GIL (Grupo Immobiliario del Lago), and the national one is AMPI (Asociación Mexicana de Profesionales Immobiliario). Stick with the agencies that belong to these organizations, and ask your agent how long he/she has been in the real estate business in this area, how he/she was trained, and any other questions that will give you assurance of credibility. Incidentally, very few people take legal action in Mexico, so just an absence of lawsuits is not sufficient proof of credibility.

There is, actually, an organization that performs oversight over individuals who represent third parties with banks and stock brokerages, where the individual is obligated to pass difficult exams in Spanish, as well as have their credit report checked. This association is the AMIB (Asociación Mexicana de Intermediarios Bursátiles). You might want to ask your bank, brokerage house, or mortgage agent about their certification.

The only class of lawyers authorized to prepare real estate deeds and documents in Mexico is a *Notario Público*, who will research and prepare your title and all the documents involved in the sale or financing transaction. See the Appendix for more information about Mexican lawyers. I can recommend Notaria 5 to you. That's located in the orange stucco building at 245-D Hidalgo (that's the *carretera* –the main road) in Chapala. It's in the block just west of the main intersection of Hidalgo and Madero streets. They speak English there, and are very easy to work with. The phone number is 376-765-2740.

Renting, at least for the first six months or so, may be your best option, however.

Reason #1: You won't be buying until you've had a chance to get the feel of different neighborhoods over time, and about the ways Mexican houses are different than the ones you're used to. Some neighborhoods are noisier than you may be used to, which is a common complaint of expats here. In some neighborhoods, people live fairly closely to each other, some have noisy guard-dogs, and some have restaurants with live music at night. Some neighborhoods have an abundance of roosters who are confused about when dawn really begins, and some have churches whose bells ring and whose loudspeakers start up at inconvenient hours.

And, parking and traffic are can be troublesome in some neighborhoods during the more crowded snowbird season. These are not show-stopping issues, however, since expats do live there, and most love it. Most just learn to live with them. But it's good to be aware of issues up front when you're choosing a place to live. Over time, the roosters, the church bells, the music, and the dogs simply blend into the tapestry of every day, just like the beautiful bird songs, the calls of the street vendors, the occasional mariachi band practices, and the cicada chirps announcing the coming of the rainy season (June through October).

On the other hand, you may want to consider whether one of the gated communities here, consisting primarily of other expats, would be right for you. These communities come with a few extra costs and rules for security and maintenance, and you may not get the flavor of Mexico you were looking for in these neighborhoods. You may feel too insulated, and the houses may look too much like the cookie cutter suburban houses you didn't like north of the border. But maybe you did like them, and maybe you would prefer a more familiar, secluded environment. All of these are trade-offs that take time to consider before buying a house.

Reason #2: Renting frees up your time. Home ownership involves a lot of effort, responsibility, time, and money. If you're downsizing, consider "letting go" of home ownership. That's what I did. I loved my home and being a homeowner in the US, and I love my home and not owning it here.

Reason #3: Rental costs are comparatively low. A nice 2-bedroom rental house (*casita*) or apartment can still be found for around $600 (and even less in some neighborhoods). You'll need to pay for your first month's rent, last month's rent, and a month's security deposit up front. But nobody will look up or care about your US credit history. That's freeing in itself. This is the land of new beginnings. All they need to see for identification is your passport.

Reason #4: Most rentals come fully furnished (or there might be an unfurnished option). When you relocate to this area, you will most likely not move all your belongings with you at first. It's comforting to know that you can take your time with the rest of your move – or that you can buy new furnishings as you find the ones you want – on your own schedule.

Reason #5: You will learn some invaluable information about Mexican houses before you actually invest in one. You will learn all about water tanks, water pressure, water purification systems, window types, ventilation, heating and cooling, insects, security, roofs, and plumbing types.

Reason #6: You will learn which real estate agencies are respected in the area through word of mouth. They're not necessarily the ones that advertise the most.

I recommend that you rent through a rental agency. They're fluent in English, and can help you in many ways as a newcomer. Plus, they're quite responsive regarding upkeep and repairs. They have repair people on staff or contracted that are competent and trustworthy – and they even speak a little English. You'll want to check online for the most prominent rental agencies in this area, and telephone. I can personally recommend one of these agencies to you: Ajijic Rentals. Be aware that in Mexico, landlords are not obligated to fix or upgrade anything unless there's a health or sanitation hazard. So, do make sure that your lease specifically states who is responsible for what, and what is included – especially if you rent from an independent landlord.

> *"Be aware that in Mexico, landlords are not obligated to fix or upgrade anything unless there's a health or sanitation hazard."*

Your Exploratory Trip: During Your Trip

Also, get a detailed list of the furnishings that are included with the house – a photographic representation is even better. Some agents "dress up" the house to rent it, but when you get there, the furniture is different, or perhaps there's a phone with no phone line.

And, do be candid about whether you'll be living with any pets. You'll find that landlords are much more accepting of pets here than they are north of the border, but there are some communities that do have pet (and children) restrictions, such as apartments and condos.

Of special interest on your lease is the subject of housekeepers and gardeners. Since most rental agencies also manage the properties, they often employ a housekeeper and/or a gardener who has worked at the house from one renter to another. Your lease should say whether your house has such arrangements, and whether those services are included in your monthly rental. Please see the Index for more information about housekeepers and gardeners.

By the way, and this is **very important**, always use your name exactly as it is spelled on your passport for all your legal documents, including your lease, house purchase, FMM and visa documents, checking accounts, and vehicle documents. Don't use only your middle initial if your passport spells it out. This could save you a lot of trouble later.

Names can be complicated in Mexico. What looks like the middle name of a Mexican native is really the father's last name. And what looks like the last name is really the mother's last name. For example, Miguel Pedro Garcia Morales's mother's last name is Morales, and his father's last name is Garcia. His middle name is Pedro.

Most Mexicans actually call themselves by their middle name. This is because parents usually use biblical saint names as the first name. It would not be uncommon for a family to have five boys whose first names are all Miguel. It's the middle name that differentiates each one. In the example above, he would probably call himself Pedro Garcia, using his middle name and his father's last name, except on legal documents.

> *"Always use your name exactly as it is spelled on your passport for all your legal documents."*

The important thing for you to remember is not to take middle names lightly – especially your own. Always make sure that no one uses your middle name mistakenly as your last name on documents.

Whether you decide to buy or rent, you'll find more housing available, and better prices, during the slow season (May through October) before the return of the snowbirds.

Your Exploratory Trip: During Your Trip

At this point, after having explored the area and available housing, and after having talked with all your contacts (agencies, B & B staff and guests, and the Lake Chapala Society), you should be able to decide whether your needs match what the Lake Chapala area has to offer. If your needs don't match, you have undoubtedly at least had an informative and interesting vacation stay. If your needs do match, *bienvenidos* (welcome)!

Once I made this decision, I felt relieved and excited and panicked all at once, and then again in waves during the following weeks. The indecision was gone, and I was ready to move full speed ahead, but I didn't know quite what that entailed. My hope is that, with this book, you will be more prepared and informed than I was.

> *"One other key activity you will want to undertake on your exploratory trip is to find a border driver."*

At this point, one of the key activities (aside from finding a place to live) you might want to undertake on your exploratory trip is to establish mailing addresses (to be used as forwarding addresses) for both letters and packages. Mexican postal system mail carriers only deliver flat mail (what they can reasonably carry) directly to your address. If there's a package, the mail carrier will give you a claim slip for it, to be picked up at the nearest post office. Many expats choose other options than delivery by the Mexican postal system, however, for many reasons. Please see the Index for additional information about mail. If, after reading about this topic, you decide you would like use the services of a mail service company, now is a good time to make those arrangements so you can provide your current home post office with forwarding addresses before your actual move.

One other key activity you will want to undertake on your exploratory trip is to find a border driver, if you want one. When most people move here from north of the border, they pack their car full of their essentials, and drive across the border. I, for one, felt a little intimidated by the prospect of then driving through half of Mexico on my own, even though I had a GPS map of Mexico. It wasn't just the armed guards at the various checkpoints that I thought might be intimidating, but the fact that I didn't know very much Spanish, or traffic rules, or which hotels allowed pets, or how to deal with potential car breakdowns or repairs.

A border driver is an English-speaking Mexican national (usually) who will take a bus to the border, meet you there, and chauffer your own car (with you in it) to your new home. He (it's always a he) can help smooth the way at the checkpoints, the toll booths and gas stations, the restaurants (he'll know the best ones on the way), hotels and rest stops. And, he'll keep you company and give you lots of additional information, too, along the way. The cost varies, and is negotiable. Your B & B staff may be able to

Your Exploratory Trip: During Your Trip

recommend a driver to you. You can certainly make these arrangements after your exploratory trip, but you might want to meet your driver first in order to feel comfortable with him.

One last important thing: be sure to take lots of photos and videos of your trip and your new home. Your friends and neighbors will be much more comfortable with your move if they can see what you've seen – a beautiful, semi-tropical lake and mountain area, populated with lots of people like yourself, enjoying their lives among a warm and friendly native population. And, if your new home is furnished, do make note of what the bed sizes are so you can bring the right size sheets.

Having said all this, I should also say that it's not strictly necessary for you to take an exploratory trip to Lake Chapala before your move. You can just drive down, find a B & B, and unload the contents of your car to a storage unit until you've found a place to live. Just Google "storage Chapala" to find a storage unit. You'll also want to ask your B & B staff about long-term off-street parking for your car within easy walking distance.

Part 2

Before Your Move

Now that you've made your decision to move to Lake Chapala, and you're back home wondering how you're going to pull it off, it might help you to know that there are really only a few main areas you need to think about at first: your finances, choosing a move date (which you may already have done), telling your family and friends, and deciding what to do about your belongings. Everything else will fall into place naturally.

Chapter 1

Consider Your Finances

There are two aspects of your finances you'll need to consider: whether you will have enough money to make the move, and whether you will have enough money to stay.

If you're moving from either Canada or the US, and you're planning to drive with your initial belongings, the whole move will most likely cost between $6,000 and $10,000. But don't panic – you will probably get that amount from the sale of your excess belongings. These figures include almost everything from your exploratory trip flight and expenses, pets (health checks), your drive down (car checkup, fuel, tolls, FMM tourist card, vehicle border deposit and permit, motel, meals, border driver), your first and last month's rent and security deposit, establishing your new insurance, utilities and technology, and buying the basics of setting up your new house (food, cleaning items, waste baskets, light bulbs).

It's after that initial outlay that you'll see the savings in your living expenses. You can stay in Mexico forever on your tourist card if you don't mind crossing the border every six months to have it and your vehicle permit re-issued for 180 more days. No one will care where in Mexico you live, or how much money you make, and you can scrape by on very little. There are decent studios, rooms, and shared housing here for as low at $275 per

Before Your Move: Consider Your Finances

month. There are also people who need house-sitters for free rent while they're traveling. And if you're frugal in everything else, you could, conceivably, squeak by on $800 per person per month. That's on paper, of course. Only you know what creature comforts you have to have as a minimum, and how long you can comfortably keep that up.

As of 2012, the government wants you to have a minimum income of 15,582.50 pesos (or the equivalent in your local currency) per person per month in order to qualify for an FM-3 visa. Spouses and economic dependents need only show 50% of that amount. Most expats here do get an FM-3 visa, so you'll want to consider this carefully.

What about working and earning money while you're here? Mexico's policies may limit a foreigner from taking a job that a Mexican could fill. But, if you do receive a job offer, you'll note that your pay will not be anywhere near what you would expect north of the border. If you accept the job offer, the hiring company will help you get a special FM-3 visa with working permission for that particular company. The

> *"As of 2012, the government wants you to have a minimum income of 15,582.50 pesos (or the equivalent in your local currency) per person per month in order to qualify for an FM-3 visa."*

working permission will be invalid if and when you leave that company.

If you move here, and work for a non-Mexican company that has a physical presence in Mexico, you will also need an FM-3 working visa, which that company will also help you obtain. Your working permission will be invalid when and if you leave that company.

If you perform any other work than what is authorized by your visa – for example, serve on a board of directors, or work for a non-profit organization without pay – you need to have authorization from immigration.

You could also work for yourself. In order to legally earn income, you need an FM-3 or an FM-2 visa, plus permission to work. If you want to hire employees, you should be aware that there's an informal policy of hiring on a 10 to 1 ratio of Mexicans to foreigners. You will need a lawyer's guidance regarding these issues, and for licenses and taxation.

Lastly, you could just work for under-the-table earnings. Lots of Mexicans do. But, you won't have the connections other Mexicans have to get away with it, and you do stand out as a foreigner. It could work out well for you, but if someone were to report you to the authorities, you could be fined and/or deported. Again, it's best to contact a lawyer (maybe on your exploratory trip) to discuss the available options for your situation.

Chapter 2

Choosing Your Move Date

Choosing your move date first may seem a little rash. But it will serve a number of purposes.

If you're planning to rent a house or apartment at Lake Chapala, you'll need to sign a lease confirming a move-in date. If you're purchasing a house, you will be negotiating a date by which you can move in. So, you will probably have come home from your exploratory trip with at least an arrival date in mind. Work backwards to arrive at a move date, depending on whether you're going to fly in or drive in.

1. Having a firm move date will focus your mind. The move will become a reality rather than a daydream – a reality whose tasks can't be procrastinated away.
2. Having a move date will strengthen your position and resolve as you discuss your move with friends and family, who may not be as excited as you are (at first).

Chapter 3

Telling Your Family and Friends

Most people I have talked to found this to be one of the most difficult aspects of the move. The first reason, of course, is that your family and friends will miss you. They're used to having you around. They would probably be upset if you moved to Paris, too, if that were the case. These are dynamics only you can address with them. You will need to soothe their fears about your relationship with them, as well as explain how the move will benefit your life in other ways. You may want to share with them the list of needs you made in making your decision, and how you feel these needs will be met. And, you'll certainly want to share with them all the photos and videos you took on your exploratory trip.

The second reason that this could be difficult is that your friends and family may have heard bad publicity about crime in Mexico. What they may not fully realize is that Mexico is a big, diverse country, and that most areas of it are not only safe, but are fascinating places to visit and live.

There are over a million expats living in Mexico (most are from the US and Canada), and many of those live in expat communities like the Lake Chapala area. These communities are composed of a blend of Mexicans and expats, and have the culture and feel of old Mexico, while growing technologically to accommodate modern needs.

Before Your Move: Telling Your Friends and Family

The major crime areas are along the northern border, and in parts of the southern Mexican states. There have been very few crimes reported involving tourists and expats – far fewer than would be experienced in, for instance, New Orleans or Chicago. The government is very happy to have expats come and spend money in Mexico without taking Mexican jobs, so they're very motivated to protect these communities. The police force responds quickly to issues that do occur – the occasional pick-pocket, or broken side mirror of a car, or a home burglary while someone is away. It's very rare that an expat gets hurt.

In this community, there are poor people living alongside well-to-do people. Sometimes the temptation to steal is overwhelming, especially if expensive-looking jewelry is worn or money is flashed imprudently. In general, I have found the Mexicans in this community to be friendly, conservative, helpful, hard-working, and very patient with all the small faux-pas we northerners inadvertently commit regarding their language, social etiquette, and customs. They also appreciate our economic impact on their charities, infrastructure, and quality of life.

You might ask your family and friends to do some additional internet research on the subject of expats living in Lake Chapala. The Appendix has a list of web boards, forums, and blogs. And, lastly, you might also find a way to involve them in some way in your move, and to invite them to come and visit you in your new home.

Chapter 4

What About Your Pets?

I need hardly say that, to most people, pets are like family. It's difficult to imagine our lives without them – once we have them. If you have been contemplating getting a new pet, wait until you get to your new home. You'll find many wonderful dogs, cats, horses, and birds of all ages in the Lake Chapala area ready to be adopted. There will undoubtedly be some stress in your household as you plan and conduct your move, and when you move in. The additional tasks and changes involved with having a new pet will only be more stressful for your household and the pet during this time.

> *"Dogs and cats are not quarantined when they come into Mexico if they are in good health."*

The Lake Chapala area has a good selection of excellent veterinarians, very good pet foods (many US brands), and very good services (grooming and boarding). I'll describe the best ways to transport your pets, which paperwork is needed, and what you can expect at the border, in future sections.

Here are some considerations to help you make pet decisions at the outset.

Before Your Move: What About Your Pets?

1. Dogs and cats are not quarantined when they come into Mexico if they are in good health, and if they have the right paperwork (more on that later).
2. You're not allowed to bring in more than three pets per person, technically. Otherwise customs MAY decide that you're in business to sell them in Mexico, in which case you will need to pay import duties on them. A reasonable number of pets isn't usually questioned, however, especially if you have other signs that you're actually moving to Mexico. To be safe, do not exceed the maximum of three pets per person, as listed on the health certificates. Three more pets could be owned by another adult in the car, though.

    "There is an automatic 30-day quarantine for all live birds going into the US."

3. Only you know whether taking your pet on a long trip is in its best interest, and yours. If your pet is very old or on extensive medical treatments, you may want to delay your move rather than risk your pet's ability to withstand the move, or to be able to adjust to a new environment.
4. Reptiles (snakes, lizards) are not allowed to cross the border (except on their own). However, some turtles have been known to be let in (with health certificates).
5. Birds are technically not considered pets for the purpose of bringing them across the border.

They're considered imports. Bringing birds into Mexico that are native to Mexico is prohibited, per a 2008 law. These include some parakeets, some macaws, and some parrots. For an up-to-date list, contact Jose Garcia at US Fish and Wildlife in Laredo, Texas. Phone number: 956-286-9961 or 956-726-2234.

6. Be aware that bringing birds back into the US is not easy, due to the many problems the US has had regarding smuggled birds – to say nothing of the bird flu and Newcastle disease scares. US customs officials do not distinguish between parakeets and chickens. They're all birds. The paperwork is extensive, and there is an automatic 30-day quarantine for all live birds going into the US. If you don't want your birds to be quarantined, you will need to give away or sell your birds in Mexico, if you decide to move back to the US later.
7. There are also restrictions on bringing birds back into Canada that you'll want to consider. Here is more information: http://tinyurl.com/9ujege3.
8. Horses are not considered pets, and, as such, must be imported through a customs broker. Here is further information: http://tinyurl.com/8ozpvm9.

The Mexican government has posted some information about bringing various pets into Mexico here: http://tinyurl.com/9ybgwpb. If you want to speak to a Mexican wildlife official, call the Secretary of the Interior's Office at 555-905-1013 or 555-905-1020.

Chapter 5

What To Do About Your House

If you rent your home, all you need to do is notify your landlord in writing when you plan to vacate your home. The amount of lead time you need to give your landlord will be noted in your lease.

If you own your home, you have four options, and they're more complicated.

Selling your house
This is the most logical option, of course. Since it may take a long time to sell, you may want to choose a real estate agent who is also willing to manage the property for you after you've moved. That way, prospective buyers won't be put off by seeing a tangle of long weeds where there should be a neat lawn. If you owe more on the house than it's worth on the market, you may qualify for what's known as a "short sale" (in the US, anyway), whereby the bank agrees to allow you to sell the house outright for less than you owe on it. Some banks are much more lenient in this regard than others. Be aware, though, that the "short sale" option does lower your US credit rating to some extent, if that's important to you. Your real estate agent can give you more information about this option. The benefits of selling your house are that you'll be able to get out from under it, and you may even end up having enough money to

purchase a house in Mexico – a much nicer house for the money, in fact.

Renting your house
This could be a good option if you think you might return to your home country to live, and if the house would still be a good fit for you at that time. A big Victorian house with 3 stories wouldn't be good for an older couple who might have difficulty with stairs, for instance. The amount you could rent the house for should be more than enough to cover your mortgage payment, all upkeep and maintenance, and the cost of an ongoing property manager. Don't take this option if your ONLY reason is to wait to sell it until the housing market bounces back. My own real estate agent advised me against this, saying the housing market won't bounce back to its 2008 level for another 10 years, at least. It's better to just get out from under the burden now, and to start fresh in your new environment.

Donating your house
If you own your house outright, and you're having trouble selling it, you can donate it to a non-profit organization in order to get a tax credit, instead. The non-profit organization can then fix up the house, and sell it later for its own charitable works.

Walking away
This option is one that many homeowners are taking when they owe more on their mortgage than the house is worth on the market, and when they are willing to sacrifice their

Before Your Move: What To Do About Your House

US credit rating for the next 7 to 10 years. Mexicans don't care about your US credit rating because most transactions are paid in cash. But walking away from your house could affect your ability to get financing for a Mexican house if the financing comes from the US (or your home country). It would certainly also affect you if you were to return to your home country within those 7 to 10 years (whether you buy or rent, or wanted to buy a car, for instance.). This one's a difficult decision. You may want to talk this over with your mortgage holder, a real estate agent in your home country, and a real estate agent in Mexico for all the implications.

Chapter 6

What About Your Car?

Should you take your car or buy one in Mexico? In general, if you're coming from the US or from Canada, it's best to take your car and drive it across the border. For other countries, it may not be worth having your car shipped to Mexico.

Only one car, SUV, RV motor home, or pickup truck (including a motorcycle carried in the bed, or on an attached trailer) **per person** is allowed in order to obtain a temporary vehicle permit. The only exception is that a vehicle being towed by an RV motor home may be owned by the same person that owns the RV motor home. Aside from that, if you're a couple, and you want to bring in two vehicles, make arrangements for the other vehicle to be temporarily imported by the other person.

> *"Most people from north of the border drive across the border in their current car."*

A new car usually costs more in Mexico than in the US or Canada because of import taxes, unless the car was made in Mexico. Plus, there's a 16% national sales tax in the state of Jalisco (border areas may have lower tax rates.). For (Mexican-plated) used cars, the pricing depends on the economy. In a bad economy, you can get very good deals –

Before Your Move: What About Your Car?

plus the 16% sales tax. Otherwise, you can expect to pay approximately 20% more for a used car than in the US. But, if you were to sell your current car in the US or in Canada with the thought of buying a Mexican-plated car once you arrive in Lake Chapala, then you would have to find another way to bring your possessions into Mexico, which would probably be more expensive than just driving in your current car. Most people from north of the border drive across the border in their current car.

If your car mechanic says your current car is on its last legs, though, get a different one that will withstand the trip, but don't get a brand new one. That's because you can't sell a foreign-plated car in Mexico (unless you have a very clever lawyer), and it's very expensive and complicated to exchange foreign plates for Mexican plates. So, plan on driving your (foreign-plated) car into the ground in Mexico because the only thing you'll be able to do with it is to surrender it to *Hacienda* (the Mexican treasury), or to drive it back into the US to sell it.

Chapter 7

What About Your Other Belongings?

This might seem overwhelming at first, but, trust me, it all falls into place as time goes on. And, you'll even become more accepting of letting things go, too. This is a great time to simplify your life, and to downsize. Possessions will seem much less important to you in Mexico, and friends, experiences, and beauty and nature will become much more important. For now, just categorize your major possessions. If you're computer savvy, build an Excel spreadsheet. Here are some high-level categories.

1. To give to family and friends
2. To take to Mexico
3. To ship to Mexico
4. To sell
5. To donate to charity
6. Not sure yet

Give to family and friends
If you're planning to leave items to anyone in your will, consider doing that now, instead. You're probably not going to need (or even want) your extensive jewelry collection, your 32 place settings of sterling flatware, or grandma's trunk of lace doilies. In fact, you probably won't need anything that's in your attic, including all your winter clothes.

Before Your Move: What About Your Other Belongings?

Take to Mexico

After you've come close to determining which things to give to your family and friends, you'll know which items are left. Here's where you need to make a big decision: whether to take only what you can ship or fit into your pick-up truck, RV, car or SUV, and get rid of everything else, or to (eventually) bring all your remaining possessions to Mexico.

Using an international moving company to move a 3 bedroom household of furniture by truck from midwest US to Lake Chapala will cost about $15,000. Only you know whether that's worthwhile for you. You can buy an awful lot of furniture in Mexico for that amount.

"Using an international moving company to move a 3 bedroom household of furniture by truck from midwest US to Lake Chapala will cost about $15,000."

And, keep in mind that your King Louis XIV chairs may look out of place in a more rustic setting. If you'd like an estimate of your moving costs, there are companies that are very good and experienced at this. One is Strom – White Moving Company (www.strommoving.com). Another is Lake Chapala Moving (www.lakechapalamoving.com). You can find others on the internet, as well. Another option you may want to ask your moving company about is shipping your possessions by boat if you currently live along a coast. That may be less expensive.

53

Be aware, though, that moving companies sometimes give very low estimates in order to get the winning bid, but then come up with creative fees at the end of the trip. It's best to eliminate very low bids for that reasons, or to put a maximum amount (say, 10%) of overage fees right into your contract. You'll also want to ask about tips for the crew. Sometimes they're mandatory. Do read the fine print in the moving contract.

Another option is to have your things moved into a storage space near the US – Mexican border. Then, whenever you or your friends and family cross the border in the future, more things can be brought down, usually without paying import duties. It's a lot more effort and time, of course, but it may be worth it to you.

Most people I've talked to decided to take only what they could fit into their pickup truck, RV motor home, SUV, or car – and to ship some bulky items, like books. You'll be surprised how much your car or SUV can hold. You could even add a (locking) roof carrier to the top (not for pets, though). Identify now which items have strong meaning for you that you can't imagine living without. In this category would be family letters and photos, memorable trinkets, your favorite guitar, and favorite books (more about books later) – and, of course, your pets and your valuable documents. You might want to get an expandable plastic file folder now, and start collecting your valuable documents in it. Don't forget the contents of your safety deposit box.

Before Your Move: What About Your Other Belongings?

In addition to taking your favorite items, you'll also want to take items that are hard to find or more expensive in Mexico. Among these are electronics. They're more expensive here because they have to be imported. The electrical plugs are exactly the same as in the US and Canada, including the 3-pronged grounded ones. So, do take (or buy now) a nice flat-screen TV, your DVD player, and your DVR.

DVRs aren't really used here, and are extremely hard to find, since there's no schedule coding of programs. You could certainly use the one you have for taping on a timed basis, though.

And, be aware that DVDs and DVD players are coded for specific regions of the world. For instance, Canada and the US are Region 1, and Mexico is Region 4. You might want to check your DVD player and DVR documentation to see which regions they support. All the pirated DVDs here do seem to be able to be played on US DVD players, though.

> *"DVRs aren't really used here, since there's no schedule coding of programs."*

If you're a computer user, you'll want to bring a nice laptop, and an all-in-one printer/copier/fax/scanner. You could also bring your wireless land phones. If you sew, you'll want to bring your sewing machine. If you have a good tool collection, bring that, too.

By the way, in order to prevent customs agents at the border from charging you duty fees on new electronics, take new items out of their boxes, and smear a little peanut butter on the cords to make them look used.

> *"To prevent customs agents at the border from charging you duty fees on new electronics, take new items out of their boxes, and smear a little peanut butter on the cords to make them look used."*

You could also bring your favorite set of dishes, cookware set, and flatware, plus your favorite kitchen gadgets. Be aware that Mexico's units of measure are in metrics. For example, pitchers here have markings for liters, not quarts. You won't need to bring your microwave, coffee maker, toaster oven, or any other small kitchen appliance, except maybe your favorite Cuisinart. Most small kitchen appliances are readily available here, and are not very expensive.

Do bring your favorite bed sheets in the correct size for your new beds. Sheets are not easy to find here, and the ones you can find are not very good quality. The same goes for bath towels. Most Mexican houses do not have a lot of carpets and rugs, so you probably won't need your vacuum cleaner. What they do have is tiles – miles and

Before Your Move: What About Your Other Belongings?

miles of tiles, which are nice and cool in this semi-tropical climate.

Of course, you'll want to decide which jewelry to bring. You'll really only use the simplest of jewelry. No one wears large cocktail rings, rhinestones, and flashy bling here. Do bring your favorite conservative, classy pieces (especially natural stones, like turquoise), and consider giving away or selling the rest. Costume jewelry is best.

Regarding clothing, you'll want to take only summer clothing, including a couple of sweaters and jackets for cool evenings. You can safely give away or donate everything else.

If you think that all of these items won't fit in your SUV, they ALL fit in my Jeep along with two big boxes of photos, two cats, a cat carrier, two medium dogs, two dog beds, and three 12-packs of Diet Dr. Pepper – all without a rooftop carrier.

Ship to Mexico

Consider shipping items to Mexico that are too big or too numerous to fit in your vehicle.

There is a US mail category specifically for shipping books internationally. It's called USPS Airmail M-Bags. It's not cheap, but it is less expensive than regular international shipping methods. You pack your books in your own boxes so that they're less than 66 lbs each. Each box must be labeled as if you were going to ship it by itself. Then, take the boxes to a post office approximately 3 weeks before your move (they'll take from 4 to 6 weeks to arrive), and they'll be put in canvas bags and tagged. The 2012 cost to Mexico is $31.35 for a bag weighing 11 pounds or less, plus $2.85 per additional pound up to 66 pounds. So, it's about $188 for a 66 pound bag – about $3.00 per pound. Here is more information about shipping your books via Airmail M-Bags: www.usps.com/send/airmail-mbags.htm. If you're not in the US, check with your post office about any special international book mailing services from your home country.

Another category of items is paintings. You'll want to pack them carefully in your car, if you can, but you may also want to ship some of them. If you decide to do that, the paintings must be quite valuable to you. In that case, I'd recommend that you have a professional crate them for you for shipping, with wood or light metal panels on the sides for protection. Don't count on the crates being babied along the route. No matter how much you label them "Fragile – handle with care", they're going to be treated nonchalantly. Compare the shipping rates between major freight carriers like Federal Express, UPS, and DHL – and have the paintings insured.

There are many excellent artists in this area, doing fascinating work, so do consider that you'll want to add Mexican art to your home. Minimize the number of art pieces and paintings you bring to the bare minimum.

Before Your Move: What About Your Other Belongings?

Sell

This will probably be your largest category of items. You might be tempted to just have a big yard sale, but that will not be the best option for most of your items unless you're in a hurry and just want to get rid of everything, taking anything left over to a charity.

If you have any unique or valuable pieces, consider auctioning them on eBay, if you know how to do that. Be sure to set an appropriate minimum dollar amount so you don't regret selling it if you only get the minimum bid. And do start the process early enough so that you will have time to try auctioning it several times.

If eBay is not a good option for you, your next-best option is to have your items auctioned by professional auctioneers. Telephone two of the most reputable auction houses in your area (just Google "auction" and the name of your city), and have them come to your house to see what you have to sell. Make sure that they deal in general household furniture, rather than just antique items. Also make sure they're registered, insured, and bonded. And, make sure that they take bids from prospective bidders by phone. That opens up the bidding to long distance and international buyers. What auctioneers will do is sell your items for you for about 30% of the total selling price. They'll do that by either moving your items to their auction house and conducting an auction there along with other peoples' items, or by having what's known as an estate auction.

> *"You might be tempted to just have a big yard sale, but that will not be the best option for most of your items unless you're in a hurry and just want to get rid of everything, taking anything left over to a charity."*

An estate auction is conducted at your house, and is done if you have a large number of items to sell, and if you have decorated your house in such a way as to display the items to their best advantage. There are positives and negatives to each type of auction. In both cases, the auctioneers will take photos of your items, and post them on their websites. The photos are then looked at by prospective buyers – around the world in many cases. This is why you'll get better prices than at a yard sale, where your buyers are usually just the people in your neighborhood.

For an estate sale, you'll probably save a little money by not having to pay for the auctioneers to move your items to their facility. But, you will have lots of company for awhile. The auctioneers will come first to price and tag everything, and then, usually over the course of a weekend, you'll get a parade of people coming through your house, which doesn't appeal to everyone. You can either be there or not. If you're there, be prepared to hear positive and negative comments about your house, your yard, your taste, and the quality and value of your items. Whether you're

Before Your Move: What About Your Other Belongings?

there or not, you'll need to make other arrangements for your children and pets on those days.

Some thefts do occur at estate auctions because the items will be located throughout your house without the security cameras that auction houses have at their own facilities. Extra staff for monitoring each room may be offered, or not. But the staff is not well paid, so that in itself could be a problem. Or, you could have your own friends and relatives monitor the various rooms, too. You will then have buyers carrying their new treasures out of your house into their waiting pickup trucks, scratching your walls and stepping on your rose bushes (you may not care at this point, though).

> *"There's less chance of theft in the auctioneer's facility because of the security cameras and the locked display cases."*

Another negative to having an estate auction in your home is that strangers will see what else you have in your home, so you may feel a little vulnerable after that. Despite these negatives, lots of people choose this option because the items are not competing with other peoples' items for attention, and may get higher prices by being shown in a warm home environment. You can choose what to do with the items that are left over after the weekend's sale.

If you have the auction in the auctioneer's facility, many of the estate auction negative considerations disappear. You will have your near-empty house to yourself, after paying the auctioneers to move the items to their facilities. This arrangement is really called consignment. You're paying them a fee to sell your items. Again, you can choose whether to be present at the auction or not. There's less chance of theft in the auctioneer's facility because of the security cameras and the locked display cases. More people may show up because there will be other peoples' items up for bidding, too. However, your items will be competing for their attention and their spending dollars. Regarding theft in either scenario, the auctioneers should be insured, so you will be reimbursed, but maybe not at the auction price you were hoping for. Whatever doesn't sell on the auction day is usually grouped together in lots and sold on another day with lower starting bids until everything is gone. This is good in that everything gets sold, but bad in that you don't have control of these remainders any more. You may have been able to sell the remainders yourself at a yard sale for more. But again, you may not care so much at this point.

> *"It's illegal to ship or mail used clothing into Mexico."*

In either scenario, you'll get a check for 2/3 of the total winning bids in about a week after the auction. If you're going to be gone by then, make sure you give the auction house your new address, or the address of someone you trust who can deposit the check in your bank account, avoiding the lengthy travel time and hold a Mexican bank would place on an out-of-country check (between 10 and 15 business days).

Auction houses usually do not take clothes, except for furs, in some cases. There's just not a great market for used clothes (at least in the US), so these will sell best at a local consignment shop (if you have the time to wait for them to sell), or at a yard sale. Or donate them to a non-profit organization for a tax deduction. Do not ship them to Mexico, whether for yourself or to donate to a Mexican charity. It's illegal to ship or mail used clothing into Mexico.

Your last option to sell is, of course, having a yard sale. Not much needs to be said about this, since you've probably done it before, and there are lots of good articles on the internet about how to have a successful one.

Donate to charity

You've probably donated clothes and small articles to Goodwill and Salvation Army (in the US) all along. But do also consider donating to local shelters and food banks. They can sometimes use old shelves, paint, tools, bags, garden equipment, decorative items (posters, prints), kitchenware, and many other items you may not have thought of. Call a few of them and ask if they have lists of needed items. You'll feel great about having made these donations whether or not you receive a tax deduction.

Chapter 8

Four Weeks Before Moving

Up until this time, you've been planning and making decisions. But now you'll need to be on a countdown because some activities need to get started now. In fact, I would say that you could accomplish your entire move in one month from when you made the decision to move to the actual moving day, if you're in a hurry. If you're at all inclined to make lists, now is the time to develop an Excel spreadsheet (if you haven't already made one) in order to stay organized and on schedule. You'll be much less stressed, and you'll be confident that you haven't forgotten anything.

If you rent your home, you should provide written notice to your landlord now (if you need to give 30 days' notice). You'll also want to make arrangements for any inspection, and for the return of your security deposit. If you own your home, you will have made a decision about your house by this time. It should be listed for sale or rent now, or arrangements should be finalized to donate it.

Now is also the time to ship or give to your family and friends the items you have decided to give them. Then, contact one or two good consignment shops (you can find them online) to determine which clothes might be worth trying to sell. Start selling them now. Also, give your home a preliminary clean-out. Get rid of junk and piles of old newspapers.

If your finances are complicated, it's a good idea to have a talk now with your accountant about how to tie up loose ends and/or manage your assets when you're in Mexico. You will also want to make sure that your will is up to date.

"You'll also want to inquire whether your bank has an arrangement with any Mexican banks to use their ATMs here without a transaction fee (which is usually $2.50 USD or so)."

For basic banking, many people just use their existing home bank debit or credit cards to withdraw pesos from ATMs in Mexico. ATMs automatically provide the best currency exchange rate. If that's what you'd like to do, keep in mind that you'll need to make a bank wire transfer to Mexico for any amounts larger than your daily maximum credit card withdrawal amount (which you might want to see if you can increase). There's a bank fee (around $15 USD) for a wire transfer. This is the simplest arrangement, provided your credit card is a common type such Visa, Visa Plus, MasterCard, Cirrus, or Pulse.

You'll also want to inquire whether your bank has an arrangement with any Mexican banks to use their ATMs here without a transaction fee (which is usually $2.50 USD or so). Bank of America, for instance, has an arrangement that allows free ATM transactions at Santander and Scotiabank ATMs here. In any case, try to get two copies of your ATM card in case one gets lost.

You can only open a bank account in most banks in Mexico if you have an FM-3 or FM-2 immigration visa (see the Index for more visa information). If you know you're going to apply for an FM-3 visa when you're in Mexico, you may want to open an account in your home country with a bank that links directly to a Mexican bank online. That way, you can transfer your money back and forth between countries easily – usually online.

"You can only open a bank account in Mexico if you have an FM-3 or FM-2 immigration visa."

One such bank is Banamex USA (owned by Citigroup). They have a special money market account (interest-earning) for US retirees called an Amistad account, whereby you can direct Social Security to deposit your monthly benefit dollars into that account (you don't have to do that right away – just open the account), and then when you get an FM-3 visa, you can open a Banamex (Mexico) account in the Lake Chapala area. Those two accounts can be linked so you can transfer money back and forth yourself online in a matter of minutes. Other banks that may have similar arrangements are BBVA Bancomer USA, HSBC, Santander, and Scotiabank. In any case, if you think you might want to have such a banking arrangement, now

Before Your Move: Four Weeks Before Moving

is the time to open such an account in your home country. It's always a good idea to have more than one source of funds, too, in case one credit card needs to be replaced, for instance.

As soon as you get to Mexico, you'll want to at least know how to count and to understand spoken numbers in Spanish. It comes up surprisingly quickly, and you'll be glad you took some time to learn the numbers in advance. Many prices are negotiable in Mexico, and you won't want to overpay just because you don't understand what a vendor is saying. Most vendors are honest, but a few might be inclined to increase prices if they suspect you won't know the difference between a quote of 800 pesos and 80 pesos. So start learning your Spanish numbers now in your spare time. Buy some index cards, and make flash cards (English on one side, Spanish on the other) of the numbers found on this video: http://video.about.com/spanish/How-to-Count-in-Spanish.htm. Practice them until you know them by sight and sound, and can say them, too. Translate in both directions. Don't worry too much about precise pronunciation at this point. They sound pretty much like they look, except that Vs are pronounced like Bs. So, *veinte* (twenty) is pronounced "bayn'tay". Learn the hundreds, too, up to a thousand (mil). This is one of those activities that you might think is not very important right now. But, please trust me on this, you'll regret not doing it. I did.

Now is also the time to think about health insurance. There is much to be said on this subject later, but for now, it's important to know two things: 1) that US Medicare does not extend to Mexico (yet), and 2) that if you choose private health insurance in Mexico (and that's what I advise), there will be a 60-day waiting period. What's important now is that you don't cancel your existing health insurance, but make sure that it stays active at least 60 days after your move date (preferably 90 days, if you can afford it). You'll want to check with your health insurance provider as to how they handle emergency benefits while you're on "vacation" in Mexico. If anything catastrophic were to happen to you within the 60 day waiting period for your new insurance, you would probably need to pay medical expenses at the time of treatment, and then submit a reimbursement claim, saying you were on a Mexican vacation (whether or not you choose to go back to the US for further treatment).

> *"Mexican law does not require you to have car insurance, but the state of Jalisco does."*

Mexican law does not require you to have car insurance, but the state of Jalisco does. And, it would be utter folly not to have it since it is relatively inexpensive, and it could prevent you from being held in police custody until all liability is paid in full (see the Index for Car Insurance). Check now with your car insurance company to find out if driving in Mexico is covered by your policy. Just as

Before Your Move: Four Weeks Before Moving

important is whether there would be an agent available (24/7) to come to the scene of an accident in Mexico, which almost never happens with US companies. This is how things are done here. The insurance agent (or a sub-contracted agent) must show up at the scene of an accident to represent you and to take financial responsibility, even if you have proof of insurance.

One of the most important things you will need to do if you are married is to have an acceptable validation of your marriage license. My lawyer told me a sad story of a Canadian expat couple in Mexico. The husband had a heart attack and died. The wife could not prove she was the lawful spouse because her marriage certificate had not been certified, so she could not claim responsibility for the body. She had to get her marriage license certified in Canada by mail and courier, which took 2 weeks at a cost of $900 in fees and services. The moral of the story is: do it now before you leave. If you are in the US, a certified document is called an apostille, and costs between $8 and $32 at your state's Secretary of State office. You can get an apostille of many different types of documents that may pertain to you (adoption papers, birth certificates). Here's a website for information: http://tinyurl.com/9oswel9. In Canada, it's called "legalizing" a document, and the fee is

"One of the most important things you will need to do if you are married is to have your marriage license certified."

69

nominal. However, it is very difficult to do it from outside of Canada, so it's important to do this in advance. See this website for more information: http://tinyurl.com/8exy52r.

Start now to collect all your important papers in one location, preferably in a portable vinyl/plastic file folder that you'll carry with you across the border. Include at this point (there'll be more later):

- Passport
- Social Security card
- Social Security retirement benefit statement
- Investment documents
- Mexican house lease or purchase papers
- Next of kin and emergency numbers

Also include these documents, which need to be apostilled or legalized.

- Birth certificate
- Certified marriage license/civil union document
- Divorce papers
- Adoption papers

Chapter 9

Three Weeks Before Moving

The next items to go into your portable file folder are your health records. In Mexico, doctors, dentists, clinics, and hospitals expect you to keep (and to keep track of) your own medical records, lab results, and x-rays. This is the opposite of what is done in the US, for example, where it's frowned upon to even see your records, much less have possession of them. Here, you're in charge of your health. When you see a doctor, she'll expect you to bring any documents with you that are pertinent to your condition.

> *"In Mexico, doctors, dentists, clinics, and hospitals expect you to keep (and to keep track of) your own medical records, lab results, and x-rays."*

If and when you decide to get private health insurance, they will want to see two years' history of any significant medical conditions (heart disease, cancer, diabetes, depression). That doesn't mean they'll exclude those conditions or increase your policy rates, necessarily, but they do want to know about them in advance. So, contact each doctor you've seen in the last two years, and tell him/her that you need their written notes, x-ray reports, and lab results for the last two years. If any of the x-rays showed anything significant, see if you can get the actual x-ray in addition to the radiologist's report.

From your dentist, all you need to ask for is the most recent set of x-rays you had done, and any recent notes regarding work done. Dental records don't need to go back two years because they're not required by the health insurance companies. File all these documents in your portable file folder.

Another task to start now is to make sure all your bills are being paid automatically or online. The goal is that by the time you notify your post office of your new address, there will be little or nothing to actually forward. Review your checking account and your stack of invoices and bills to see which merchants you're still paying by mail. Some of them can be paid right on the merchant's website, instead. For the remainder, you'll want to set up online bill paying on your banks' online banking site. It's easy and reliable, and usually free. You may have written your last check – they're not used very much in Mexico.

If you have magazine subscriptions, you'll want to check whether they're available in digital format instead (on your PC or other devices). The hardcopy versions will not be forwarded internationally.

You'll also want to make note of your favorite mail-order catalogs so you can visit those merchants online later

Before Your Move: Three Weeks Before Moving

instead of waiting for their catalogs in the mail. The catalogs won't be automatically forwarded internationally.

If you live near an IKEA store, buy some of their giant blue plastic shopping bags. You'll love them for open-air flea markets (*tianguis*) here, where there are no shopping carts. Those fruits and vegetables, flowers, bakery, fish, and what-nots get heavy. You can sling one bag over each shoulder. And get some for your partner, too. You'll be glad you did. In fact, bring extra, and sell them to people who don't have any. They're much coveted here.

> *"If you live near an IKEA store, buy some of their giant blue plastic shopping bags."*

Now is also a good time to decide which books you want to take with you in your car, and which ones you want to ship. I recommend that you buy a pocket-sized Spanish/English – English/Spanish dictionary for your car. In my opinion, the best ones are the Langenscheidt versions. You can get a good used copy on Amazon.com or on eBay for under $10.

For books to be shipped, keep in mind that you'll pay approximately $3.00 per pound. Set the ones for shipping aside now, and get some boxes for them. The book boxes from moving companies like U-Haul are best because they're the right size for books, and they're heavy duty.

Pack the boxes tightly (not a lot of wiggle room), and tape them with reinforced strapping tape – not just clear shipping tape. They're going to go through a rough ride.

Label each box as if you're going to ship it separately, with the destination address and a return address. You'll want to use someone else's return address in your home country, just in case. There's no point having them returned to the address you're leaving. You can take them to the post office for M-Class shipping either this week or next. They'll take from 4 to 6 weeks to get to you in Mexico. You'll get a notice from the post office here when they're ready to be picked up.

> *"If you have a smartphone or an electronic tablet, you'll also want to install some language translation applications on them."*

Also, do contact your current cell phone carrier now to find out what to expect when you use the phone in Mexico. If it uses a 3G or 4G network, it will work in Mexico – for an added fee. It's called roaming. Find out how to turn roaming on and off on your devices for both voice and data (cell phones pass location data back and forth in the background automatically on the network), and how much extra it will cost.

Before Your Move: Three Weeks Before Moving

If you use a GPS device (Global Positioning System), you'll want to download a map of Mexico now, and to familiarize yourself with it. Most Garmin and TomTom devices have Mexican maps available.

If you have a smartphone or an electronic tablet, you'll also want to install some language translation applications on them. The first app is **Google Translate**, and it's free. It translates words between any two of 64 languages. You

> *"If you know you'll be arriving at your new home in Mexico in the evening, and you don't have your new house keys yet, you will want to make arrangements with your new landlord or real estate agent to give your driver the keys to bring with him."*

can either type the word or speak it, and it will pronounce the word for you, too. It's very handy. But it does require an internet connection – either 3G or 4G if you're out in the open, or a wireless LAN if you're in a wi-fi hotspot.

Another great application is **Word Lens**, and it's $9.99 for each set of two languages. It has two different functionalities. If you hold up your device's camera lens to a sign or document, it will translate the words on it in real time. It's quite amazing to see. The second functionality is a straight-forward word translation, whereby you type in a word, and it will give you all the different meanings. Word Lens does not require an internet connection, so you can use it anywhere. The only downside is that it seems to have fewer words in its memory than Google Translate. But it's well worth the price. I've used it for menus, signs at the park, contracts, and my Mexican cell phone instruction manual.

Contact your border driver this week to confirm your meeting point date and location. And, get his cell phone number in addition to his email address. This will come in handy as you're trying to locate each other at the border.

> *"If your DVD player gets lost or broken in the process of moving, you won't be able to play your unfinalized DVDs on a new player."*

Also, if you know you'll be arriving at your new home in Mexico in the evening, and you don't have your new house keys yet, make arrangements with your new landlord or real estate agent to give your driver the keys to bring with him.

By the way, be aware that Mexican cell phone numbers have a different format than you would expect. See the Index for Telephone Dialing.

And finally, you'll want to make sure that the homemade DVDs you're taking with you are "finalized" (check your user manual about how to do this). If your DVD player gets lost or broken in the process of moving, you won't be able to play your unfinalized DVDs on a new player.

Chapter 10

Two Weeks Before Moving

During this week, you will want to get a two-month supply of your normal medications. The only reason for getting that much is that you're going to be so busy with other details during the first month of moving in, you'll be glad you don't have to think about your medications, or about going to a new doctor for awhile. Most doctors and health plans will allow their patients to get a two-month supply of drugs for when they go on extended vacations.

Another task for this week is to purchase any pet carriers you may need. If you're going to fly your pets into Mexico, check with the airlines for specifications. The hard-cased carriers are almost all labeled as to whether they meet airline specifications. Just make sure your pet can stand, sit, and lay down comfortably in the size you choose. If you're going to drive dogs across the border, you probably don't need carriers. You just need a comfortable place for them to lie down. What I did was place their soft beds on top of large plastic bags of folded clothes in the back of my SUV. The bags made a nice flat surface for the beds, and added some cushioning for them, too.

Transporting cats is a little trickier, unless they're housetrained and will go to the bathroom on a leash (there are not many cats who fit this description). You probably won't want them loose in your car for fear of not only having soiling accidents, but that they'll get loose and run away when you open a door. So, you'll need a cat carrier that can contain a litter box plus food and water. What I found was a soft sided one with nylon and mesh on the sides and a full zipper at the front. I put a 13" by 9" sheet cake pan with absorbent sand in it in the back of the carrier, and the food and water along the sides. I fit two cats in there very well. You'll also want a smaller, foldable carrier just for transporting the cats up and down from your motel room because the "car" carrier won't be strong enough to manage carrying the cats running around and the heavy sand. This arrangement, while it was time consuming to maintain, worked very well for me on the road.

During this week, you'll also want to make appointments for next week with your veterinarian for all your animals. They'll need to be brought up to date on their vaccinations, and the vet will need to certify on an international health form (make sure she has forms there) that the animals are up to date on their shots, that they're healthy, and that they don't have any parasites. If you're flying the animals across the border, the international health forms should be dated no more than 3 days before the flight (you may be able to convince your veterinarian to leave the date blank for now). If you're driving, try for no more than 10 days before you'll be crossing the border. Some sources say you have up to 30 days in advance when you're driving, but why take a chance?

Before Your Move: Two Weeks Before Moving

Regarding your home, you'll want to leave it clean for the next person moving in. So, if you can afford it, hire a cleaning person now to do that for you sometime in the last few days before your move. You'll be surprised how much there will be to clean after all your furniture is removed.

Now is also a good time to notify your post office about stopping your mail. If you live in the US, you can do it online here: http://tinyurl.com/4maqprq.

You can either provide your new Mexican address to the post office or not. If you choose not to, all mail (except junk mail, which will be discarded) will be returned to the sender. By this time, you should have notified everyone you want to what your new address is.

You can also tell your newspaper subscription folks now when to stop your deliveries. That can be done by phone.

And now for copies. In Mexico, it seems you need copies for almost everything. Even though almost all significant businesses have computers, they still like to have copies of transactions with your signature on them, and then they use rubbers stamps on them. Unfortunately, it's usually only stationery stores (*papelarías*) that make copies – for a peso or two. If you go to a bank, for instance, and they tell you that you need two copies of something, you might wonder why they don't just go in the back and make a few copies. It just doesn't work that way. It costs money. You will probably be directed to the nearest *papelaría* (if you ask), and then you'll have to come back again. That's why you'll be very glad you've brought your own all-in-one printer/copier/scanner/fax.

In fact, it will be easier to make some copies now (before you move) of some documents that require internet access (which might take a little while to re-establish after you move). If you're planning to file for an FM-3 (retirement) visa (see visas in the Index), you'll need to show the most recent 3 months' bank statements. The account to choose, if you have more than one, is the one showing your Social Security benefit (or other retirement fund) deposits. So, make at least one copy of the last 3 months' transactions. If you're getting regular retirement benefits, also make a copy of the document the agency sent you, showing your monthly benefit amount and the starting date. Again, those copies will be for getting your FM-3 visa. You might as well file them in your folder now.

For your border crossing into Mexico, you'll need other copies for your file. You'll want 3 copies of:

- your passport (the face page)
- your driver's license
- your car registration
- your car title
- your pets' international health documents

One last item: you could get a haircut now, so you won't have to think about it again for awhile. However, haircuts are less expensive at Lake Chapala.

Chapter 11

One Week Before Moving

This is the last week of getting rid of all the things that you won't be taking with you. You might want to start a pile in one area of the house with everything you're going to take in the car. You can start packing clothes now, but you won't want to unplug your computer, TV, and phones until the last day, of course.

You'll want to clean out the clutter from your car this week, and take it for a mechanical inspection at your local repair shop. Make sure all the fluids are topped off, including windshield wiper fluid. Also, make sure they fill the tires with air at the correct pressure, that the tires are in good shape, and that you have a good spare tire.

"Print out a copy of the Jalisco and federal driving laws located in the Appendix."

Also print out a copy of the Jalisco and federal driving laws located in the Appendix. Put this document in your glove compartment for reference later, in case there are ever any questions about laws or fines. Some police officers here are not completely familiar with them.

At home, use up the groceries in your refrigerator, pantry and cabinets. If you have time, donate what you won't be using to a local shelter or food bank.

Be aware that any medications that don't have a prescription label are considered contraband, no matter how innocuous the medication is. It's a very serious crime to bring drugs like pain medications and amphetamines into Mexico which have not been issued by prescription.

"Call your bank, and advise them that you're going to be traveling so they won't decline transactions when they see unusual locations or activities on your account."

Also, you must get rid of all weapons and ammunition before you cross the border. Make sure you don't have a single bullet anywhere – not even in the pocket of your favorite hunting jacket. You will have a small army of AK-47s escorting you to the nearest Mexican jail if you do. And you will be staying there for a long time.

Call your bank and credit card companies, and advise them that you're going to be traveling so they won't decline transactions when they see unusual locations or activities on your account. Make sure the notation will be effective for all your accounts.

Before Your Move: One Week Before Moving

Withdraw enough cash from your bank now to get you to the border. If you can, pay any hotel bills, gas, and tolls in cash in order to avoid having to deal with any suspicious charges later.

Take your pets to the vet, and have an international health certificate filled out for each of them. Also, ask to have a copy of your pets' medical records to take with you.

Then pack, pack, and pack.

On your last day before moving:

- contact your border driver, if you have one, to confirm your meeting day and time at the border,
- go to the store, and buy sandwiches, fruit, snacks, and beverages for your trip,
- make arrangements for a house walkthrough, the return of house keys, and the return of any security deposit, and
- load your car as much as possible before tomorrow.

Part 3

Your Move

"Part 3" is a fitting title here because, if you're like many expats living in Mexico's Lake Chapala area, you're in the third part of your life. This is a time for expansion and discovery, unencumbered by the relentless push to earn as much money as possible that may have entrapped you materially and spiritually in the second part of your life.

Your life will change dramatically from this point forward. Mexico is now your home, and you're on your way there. You will look back on the second part of your life with nostalgia, just as you look back on the first part of your life. You can always go back to revisit it, but you can't relive it because you will have changed.

Think of this as your great adventure.

Chapter 1

Driving to the Border

You'll want to leave early in the morning if you want to minimize the number of nights spent in motels. Just pack your car, take your pets, take your cell phone, take a camera, lock the door, and go. Don't worry about what you might have forgotten, or forgotten to do. Just make sure your pets are comfortable, and then enjoy the ride and the scenery.

You're probably going to be driving through areas you've never seen before, so you'll want to take rest stops every few hours, not only for the obvious reasons, but also to admire the new area. On one of my rest breaks, I saw an Amish horse carriage moving at quite a fast clip-clop along the highway. Even though I had read about the Amish, and had seen them on TV, I was really amazed to actually see such an old-fashioned, black, covered carriage with a tall-hatted man driving it with reigns. It was as jaw-dropping as if Abraham Lincoln had just driven by. I also saw Dollywood on another of my rest stops. It wasn't quite as inspirational, but fun, nevertheless.

Do keep in cell phone contact with a friend or relative along the way, especially if you're driving alone. You'll feel like you're sharing your adventure, and they'll be less worried about you.

Your Move: Driving to the Border

If the weather is warm, park in the shade and roll down the windows a few inches if you need to leave your pets in the car for a few minutes when you stop to get lunch. You can get your lunch to go, and eat outside with the dog on a leash, if the weather is nice.

If you've brought pets, it's good to know that all US Motel 6 motels always take them, because you'll find them everywhere. That said, Motel 6 motels are not all created equal. I found some to be surprisingly nice, and some were really not. Much depended upon how nice the town was, and how nice the particular area of the town was. All the rooms have access to the internet, so do bring your laptop to your room. And always take your portable file folder containing your important papers and copies with you into your room overnight. If there's a store close by, get some apples, crackers, and string cheese for the next day's snacks.

> *"If you've brought pets, it's good to know that all US Motel 6 motels always take them, because you'll find them everywhere."*

Also, if you plan to bring cats into your room to let them roam, make sure the room is cat-proofed first. If the base of the bed is not enclosed, the cats will have a place to hide where you will spend a long time swearing while trying to get them out. As a last resort, leave them in the car in their carrier with the windows rolled down ¼ of the way.

I found that 8 hours was about the right amount of time to drive per day without getting groggy. I always had an early breakfast in a café or pancake house while the pets were still in the motel room. Then I'd drive (with one rest break) until noon or 1 o'clock for lunch. I'd have one or two rest breaks in the afternoon, and then drive until I found a highway sign for Motel 6 around 5 o'clock, well before dark.

When you get to Laredo, or whatever border town you've chosen, you'll notice that there are lots of *"Casa de Cambio"* stores or kiosks. That's where you'll want to exchange all your money into pesos. You won't be able to use US money anywhere along your drive to Lake Chapala – not for food, not for gas, and not for tolls. You will be able to use your Visa or MasterCard, though, at many of these places (not all) – that is, if your bank doesn't decline your Mexican transactions, even though you've called them in advance to alert them. If you get declined, call your bank again and complain. They should be able to fix the problem right away. But, you might as well get enough pesos for the whole trip. You'll need enough for your driver's fee, your driver's tip (10% is good), any motel costs, restaurants on the way, gasoline, tolls, and border crossing costs.

Gasoline will cost you about $3.25 USD per gallon (at 2012 summer prices). So, figure out how many miles your trip will be, divide that by how many miles per gallon your vehicle goes on the highway, and that's how many gallons

Your Move: Driving to the Border

you'll need. Multiply that times the cost in pesos per gallon. That'll be your gasoline cost. The tolls will probably cost a total of 600 pesos. And, unless you end up paying import tax on something, your border crossing fees will probably be around $75 USD, plus a vehicle deposit of between $200 USD and $400 USD (see the Index for more information vehicle deposits).

> *"In Mexico, the US dollar sign ($) is also used for pesos, which can be confusing."*

By the way, in Mexico, the US dollar sign ($) is also used for pesos, which can be confusing. In Mexico, sixty US dollars will look like this: $60 USD. Sixty pesos will look like this: $60 MXN or $60 MXP, or simply like this: $60. In most cases, common sense will tell you which is which, but be sure to ask if you're not sure.

Chapter 2

At the Mexican Border

You'll want to cross the border first thing in the morning when you're fresh and ready for a full day. This is especially true if you have a driver who is going to take you to your new home in one day, without stopping anywhere overnight.

The first thing I noticed when approaching the Laredo border was that almost all the signs were only in Spanish. I had been used to signs being in both English and in Spanish in the US, but in Mexico (and even approaching Mexico), that's not the case. The second thing I noticed was that few of the border crossing staff spoke English. I suppose that's because most of them don't need higher education to do their jobs (like toll booth staff), but I was still surprised that they don't hire bilingual people there. Nevertheless, you'll get through it. Everybody does. Just smile, be cooperative, let them direct you, and be patient.

There are three things you will need to accomplish as you cross the border.

1. You have to get an FMM tourist card
2. you have to get a vehicle permit, and
3. you have to pass through customs.

Your Move: At the Mexican Border

In addition to these "musts", you will also want to get Mexican car insurance right away.

For all the documents you will receive and sign here, it is very important for you to make sure that your name is spelled exactly as it is on your passport, and that your middle name is not mistakenly being used as your last name.

FMM Tourist Card

If you're coming from the US or Canada, you won't need a visa to enter Mexico, but you will need an FMM tourist card. Issuance of your FMM tourist card, payment of the 294 peso fee, and issuance of the vehicle permit is done in a government building away from the main traffic flow, so you'll want to take that exit (assuming you don't already have these documents). If you miss the exit (as I did), there are staff who will notice the lack of a vehicle permit sticker in your car a little later, and they'll point you back to the right place. In my case, I still couldn't find the building, so one of the staff agreed to hop in my car and navigate me there. That worked, but he asked for $200 pesos to get back out of the car. I thought that was a bit rich, so I gave him $50 pesos, instead, and said, "Adios". He grudgingly left. I smiled at him after he was out, and he smiled and waved back. My very first Mexican experience! I laughed it off, realizing that this may just be the way they earn a little extra for their efforts. I was grateful for the help.

It is in this building that you may want to meet your border driver, if you have one. Park in the building's parking lot, and bring your portable file folder with you inside. The people there do speak English.

You'll get your FMM tourist card at the first window. Ask for the maximum time period of 180 days. What this means is that, unless you get a visa during that period of time, you will have to leave Mexico after 180 days, and cross the border again for another FMM tourist card for another 180 days. See the Index for information on visas. You will need your passport, a copy of your passport, and about 294 pesos (about $25 USD).

Vehicle Permit and Deposit

Then you'll be directed to another window to get your vehicle permit and sticker. They'll ask for your FMM tourist card, your passport, your car's original title, your car registration, driver's license, and various copies of these. Your permit and sticker will cost about 700 pesos ($50 USD) plus a deposit. Be careful to keep all your receipts. Otherwise, you may have to pay this again later.

"Your vehicle permit will be valid as long as your FMM tourist card is, which is up to 180 days."

The vehicle deposit may be paid by cash or by credit card. The deposit will be reimbursed when you take the car out of Mexico before the permit expires, or before the expiration of an extended date (if you get a visa) after properly notifying *aduana*. You may or may not get the deposit back when you surrender it to *Hacienda* (Mexican Treasury) when you no longer want the car. The amount of your deposit depends on how old it is. For 2007 or newer vehicles, the amount is $400 USD. For 2001 through 2006 vehicles, it's $300 USD. For 2000 and older vehicles, it's $200 USD.

Your vehicle permit will be valid as long as your FMM tourist card is, which is up to 180 days. See the Index for information on visas to learn about what happens to the vehicle permit when you upgrade to a visa.

<u>The half sheet of colored paper your sticker is on is your vehicle importation permit. It is almost irreplaceable, and can cause you many problems if it is lost or stolen.</u>

> *"The half sheet of colored paper your sticker is on is your vehicle importation permit. It is almost irreplaceable, and can cause you many problems if it is lost or stolen."*

Mexican Car Insurance

Just before you leave the building, you'll see areas where you can purchase Mexican car insurance. If you don't already have good Mexican car insurance (or if you don't know whether you do), sign up for the maximum coverage at any one of them for 30 days. Make sure it covers bail bonds and legal expenses. It's very inexpensive. And also make sure you know which drivers of your vehicle are insured. After you've moved in, you'll want to purchase annual car insurance at even better rates. Make sure you keep the business card in a secure place in your wallet. If you're in an accident in Mexico, calling your car insurance agent is one of the first things you'll want to do.

Just before you leave the parking lot, you'll see a booth where there are staff who will apply the vehicle permit sticker to your windshield in just the right place. If you miss the booth, you can apply the sticker yourself. It goes on the inside of the front windshield, in the center, just below your rearview mirror.

Customs

Customs (*aduana*) is for making sure you don't have contraband, and for paying import duties on high-value items and new merchandise for sale. As you near the customs area, you'll see signs to move into different lanes if you have something to declare. That would be true if you're importing something you're planning to sell, or if you have something of particular value. If what you have in your vehicle are just normal household items, your own

Your Move: At the Mexican Border

jewelry, art, and pets, you won't need to declare anything. So, you can just stay in the *"Nada que Declarar"* car lanes. You can check the following webpage to make sure that your items will be duty-free: http://tinyurl.com/c65j9pd.

You'll see that every car in the normal flow of traffic will then get a green or a red stop light. If you get a green light (and ¾ of the time, you will), you've just cleared customs, and you're good to drive into Mexico. If you get a red light, you'll just pull over to the side, and follow the instructions of the customs guards carefully. You may be asked to show your passport, the international health certificates for your pets, and answer various questions about where you're going, and why. They may ask you to remove various items for inspection, or not. In all cases, be pleasant and cooperative. You'll soon be on your way.

Chapter 3

Driving to Lake Chapala

At this point, your Mexican border driver, if you have one, will have taken over driving your car to Lake Chapala. Make sure everyone is wearing their seat belts; it's mandatory in Mexico.

One of the first things you'll notice (especially near the border) is that there will be guards, police, and sometimes Mexican military troops stationed at various points, and they'll have large rifles. You may even need to stop if there's a checkpoint. Do not become alarmed. They're there to prevent the transportation of illegal contraband – usually drugs going into the US, and weapons and ammunition going into Mexico. Just be cooperative and business-like.

"You'll want to take only toll roads (cuotas). They're very well maintained, and usually have four lanes."

This is the time to bring out your GPS, if you have one, so you can follow along on your route. If you want a map, they're usually sold at the gas stations along the way.

You'll want to take only toll roads (*cuotas*). They're very well maintained, and usually have four lanes. Non-toll

Your Move: Driving to Lake Chapala

roads (*libres* – free roads) are much less consistent because they get much less maintenance. They may be only two lanes wide with no shoulders, and they may have potholes. And, they're generally considered to be less safe.

There'll be toll booths on the toll roads, most of which (but not all) take MasterCard and Visa. The amount will be between 100 pesos and 300 pesos at each one, for a total of about 800 pesos. And keep your toll receipts handy during your drive. It pays not only for general upkeep of the toll roads, but it also includes insurance for you in case of an accident. It's very good insurance, too, paying for all costs, including all repairs and all medical bills.

> *"If you have an emergency while driving on the toll roads, call the **Green Angels (Los Angeles Verdes**), a fleet of radio dispatched trucks with bilingual crews. They can be reached by dialing **078 or 800-903-9200.**"*

If you have an emergency while driving on the toll roads, call the **Green Angels (Los Angeles Verdes**, a fleet of radio dispatched trucks with bilingual crews. They can be reached by dialing **078 or 800-903-9200.** Services include protection, medical first aid, mechanical aid for your car, and basic supplies. You will not be charged for services, only for parts, gas, and oil. Their services are paid for by the Mexican government. The Green Angels patrol daily from dawn until sunset, so try not to drive after that. If you are unable to call the Green Angels, pull off the road and lift the hood of your car. Chances are good they will find you. They come by frequently. Again, keep in mind that the toll you paid at the last toll booth includes insurance.

Part 4

Your First Month at Lake Chapala

Welcome – you're finally here! You will undoubtedly find that all your native Mexican and expat neighbors are friendly and helpful. Even if you live in a neighborhood that has mostly walled-in homes (a carry-over from Spanish hacienda and courtyard styles), as soon as you meet your neighbors (and you'll meet lots of people in the streets, stores, parks, and plazas, too), you'll be greeted warmly.

Although you'll enjoy meeting these new people, your best friends during your first months (aside from this book, of course) will probably be your landlord or agency staff. That's because they're the best ones to advise you regarding your initial utilities, food, water, and services. After your basic needs have been met, and you feel reasonably stable, you'll have more time for comparison shopping, new options, and your own explorations.

Chapter 1

Your First Week

Your first order of business, especially if you arrive at your home in the evening, is to make sure you'll be comfortable overnight, and that means water and toilet paper. Water straight from the tap is not clean enough to drink from here (for the most part). So, right after you open the front door of your new home, even before you tip your driver (about 10% of his fee) and send him on his way, head for the kitchen to see if there is any bottled water. It will either be in the refrigerator, or in a stand-alone receptacle.

Next, go into the bathroom, and make sure there is toilet paper. If you've got water and toilet paper, you won't need to go back out until the morning. Otherwise, ask your driver to take you to the nearest 7-Eleven or OXXO store (it's like a 7-Eleven) – he'll know where they are – so you can get your essentials. Both of these stores are open 24 hours a day.

By the way, the water is not so bad that you can't brush your teeth with it or wash your dishes with it. You'll ingest minimal amounts of water from those activities, and that won't give you any trouble (at least it never has for me). See the Index under Water for more information.

On your first full day, you'll probably want to go shopping for some basics to get you started. Because you'll need a broad range of items, the best place to go first is to Walmart. You'll find it similar to the Walmarts north of the border, but with somewhat fewer and different selections. Don't forget to add bottled water to your shopping list if your house doesn't have a water purification system. See the Index for Buying Groceries and for Buying Water for more information. If you don't have a local map yet, don't be afraid to ask for directions. Everyone knows where the Walmart is. Just roll down your car window as ask, *"Donde está* Walmart?" (Where is Walmart?) This assumes, of course, that you have a vehicle to drive. If you don't, please see the Index for the chapter on Getting Around.

Next, you'll want to call your real estate or rental agent or landlord to make an appointment with them. If you don't have a map, they can give you directions – or perhaps they can come to pick you up the first time. Take along a list of subjects you want to talk to them about, and then, do take notes because there will be lots of new information. Your list of subjects should include the following.

1. You'll want a list of **emergency numbers** for police, fire, and ambulance for your area. Compare them to the ones in the Appendix to make sure they're the most current.
2. Ask them if they have a local **map** you can keep.
3. Ask them if they will pay for changing all the **locks** because the previous residents (and their

friends, relatives, and household staff) may have made and kept extra keys. If they won't pay for new locks, have it done anyway, and pay for it yourself. Ask them for a reference for this service because they may get a special discount.

4. If there's a **gardener** and/or **housekeeper** associated with your house, find out their names, whether they have their own keys, and what days and times they normally come. See the Index for more information about Housekeepers and Gardeners. You'll want to ensure that you're at home the first time they arrive in order to introduce yourself.

5. You'll want to know some information about your basic **utilities**. If you're renting, you'll already know from your lease whether your electricity, tap water, and gas are included in your monthly rent. If they're not, you'll want to make sure these accounts are transferred to your name, and that you won't be paying for the previous resident's expenses. You'll also want to know how and when you're expected to pay your utility bills. Is it paid in person somewhere? If you're renting, is it paid through the agency? Whom should you call if there is a utility outage or emergency? What about on weekends? If it's the utility company itself, will there be English speakers available by phone? If you own your home, the seller or real estate agent can get all that information for you. No

deposits are required for the utilities by the utility companies, but, if your landlord is going to pay them on your behalf, he/she may want you to keep a utility reserve account with him/her. See the Index for more information about Utilities.

6. You'll also want to know about your options for **TV**, **internet**, and land **phone**. Some of them may already be installed or available in your home. For instance there may already be a particular vendor's roof-top satellite dish. That doesn't mean you have to sign up for that vendor, though. That's your decision to make. So, do ask your agency or landlord what's already installed. For more information about your choices, please see the Index under Technology.

7. If you're renting, ask for a convenient time for them to conduct a **walk-through** of the house with you to write down any existing damage so it won't be deducted from your deposit when you leave. And then, make note of which of the damages you want fixed. For instance, if there's a chip on a tile, you probably won't want to bother. You may be asked to contribute to or even pay for the costs if they are considered to be minor, and if you insist on having them fixed. Remember that in Mexico, landlords are only legally obligated to fix things that affect health and safety. However, the reputable rental

agencies in the area are very much aware that renters from north of the border have somewhat higher expectations, and they try to be accommodating.

8. Ask for a good general **handyman** reference – someone who speaks some English (if you're not confident about your Spanish). Even though you may be the handy type yourself, there's a whole world of machines, contraptions, and materials here that you've never had experience with before. Whether you own your home or you're renting, this will be an important contact person for you. Chances are that he (it's almost always a he) is already familiar with your home, and can give you excellent advice regarding upkeep and some of its quirks – and also give you advice about the best places to buy materials at low prices for your do-it-yourself projects later.

9. Ask about how much gas is left in your roof-top **gas tank**, how often it needs to be filled, and who to call to get it filled or looked at.

10. Also ask when the last time your roof-top **water tank** (*tinaco*) was cleaned out and when the filter was last replaced. It's on your roof because gravity is what gives you your water pressure. Because the town water is not as clean as it is north of the border, sediment collects in the bottom of the tank and in the filter. Depending on which town you live in, you may

need to have the tank cleaned every six months or every year, and the filter should be replaced every six months. If you rent, your landlord or rental agency usually pays for the tap water, so they will usually also pay for the *tinaco* maintenance. If not, check with your new handyman.

11. Similarly, you will need to have your ground-level water **cistern** *(aljibe)* cleaned out periodically, too. Unless you have a well, the cistern is where the town water enters your property, and is initially stored. It has an electric pump that pumps water up to the roof-top *tinaco* when it runs low. This cistern needs to be cleaned out on the same schedule as the *tinaco*. So, you'll want to know when the last time was that it was cleaned out. If this is not cleaned out often enough, not only will you be washing your dishes with water that isn't as clean as it could be, but your laundry will start to show brown spots and not smell fresh. Your handyman should also be asked to put chlorine tablets in the cistern (or you can do that yourself), but that should be in addition to, not a substitute for, the cleanings.

12. Find out about **garbage collection** in your neighborhood. How often is it collected, and when? Which materials are collected, and which are not? Where would you take the other materials? Are garbage cans required, or are

just bags OK? Where should the garbage be placed – on the curb, or someplace else?
13. You'll also want to ask now about **fumigation/extermination** for insects (spiders, cockroaches, ants, scorpions). If you're renting, your landlord or agency may pay for that initially, or at least recommend a service that does that. In either case, you'll want to ask when the last fumigation was, and what the particular bug issues were. You can also buy cans of insecticide spray at Walmart or a hardware store (*ferretería*), of course.

Once you've set an appointment with your landlord or agency to discuss the above issues, you'll want to head for the **Lake Chapala Society**. It's located in Ajijic on a street called 16 de Septiembre (that's the date of Mexico's independence). The address is 16A. Their office and services are open from 10 to 2 Monday thru Saturdays, and their grounds are open until 5. Call them at 376-766-1140, if you need directions. Or, you can visit their website at: www.lakechapalasociety.com. They're a wonderful non-profit resource for all expats, and have a range of activities, information, courses, special interest groups, lending libraries, volunteer opportunities, and social events to keep you busy full-time, if you want. Plus, their grounds are beautiful: water-lily ponds, wandering egrets, lovely gardens, a gazebo, and plenty of patio furniture to just relax and have a snack at their cafe. They have a big community bulletin board, too, with notices of all kinds: home rentals

Your First Month at Lake Chapala: Your First Week

and sales, pets for adoption, household help, items for sale, upcoming presentations on healthcare and immigration, and local events.

The first thing you'll want to do is head for the office there to learn about membership. Many of their activities and benefits are just for members, so most people do join. Then you'll want to go to the bookshop area near the café to buy some local maps. I particularly recommend two fold-out maps: the blue "Lake Chapala Maps" by Tony Burton, and the orange "Mexico Travelers Map Guide to Lake Chapala, Ajijic and Environs". I like the latter because it shows the bus routes of both the major buses and the mini buses. See the Index under Buses. You'll want to buy several of these maps so you can have them handy at home, in your car, and in your purse. You'll refer to them often.

> *"The Lake Chapala Society could become like a second home to you."*

After that, you might want to introduce yourself to the person in the information booth. That's an expat volunteer (almost everyone at the Lake Chapala Society is an expat volunteer) who has been in this area for at least two years, and can help answer any questions you may have about the area, or services, or special needs. They're there to help you – whether you're a member or not.

The Lake Chapala Society could become like a second home to you. It is to many of Lake Chapala's expats, including me. It's a friendly place to just connect with others like yourself – or to do nothing at all in a peaceful, supportive environment.

After that, you'll want to make extra house **keys**. This is particularly important if you have a walled-in back or side yard from which you can't get out unless you go through the house. The wind can easily slam the door shut and lock you out. So, keep a spare set of back or side door keys there so you never have to worry. That actually happened to me on a Sunday. I was lucky enough to have my cell phone with me, and the cell phone number of my handyman. Otherwise, I would have been stuck in my back yard for a very long time, not knowing how or who to call for help. You'll also want separate front door keys, garage keys, and car keys. And, you'll need a set of keys for your household help, as well, if they don't already have them.

There are many places to get keys made. But I recommend a particular locksmith and key store because they do a good job of filing down the metal burs, which can make the difference between the keys working smoothly or not – or not working at all – so you have to go back again to have them re-filed. It's a small, yellow shack on the corner of Revolución and the *carretera* (the main road) in Ajijic. It's called *Cerrajería Cardenas* (Locksmith Cardenas), and it's located to the east side of the Bugambilias Plaza, right next to Salvador's Restaurant.

Your First Month at Lake Chapala: Your First Week

This first week at your new home is also the best time to make your **mailing services** choices. See the Index under Mail for a full explanation. While you're near the Bugambilias Plaza getting your keys made, you'll also want to visit one of the three main mailing service stores in the area: Sol Y Luna (Sun and Moon) to ask about their services and rates. It's inside the Bugambilias Plaza. The entrance to the inside of the plaza is located in the front of the plaza (ask for directions at Salvador's Restaurant out in front – they're bilingual there). Sol y Luna is located all the way down inside the main entrance on the left. They're bilingual, too.

The above activities should keep you busy for the first week in your new home. In fact, many of these activities will keep you busy for a few weeks – maybe for a full month. You will find that they will take you longer than expected. That's because Mexico runs on Mexican time, as the saying goes – there's less of a sense of urgency here. Learn to relax, and try not to get frustrated. There's no need to hurry. Everything will get done soon enough.

Chapter 2

Your Second Week

By your second week, you'll have a fairly long to-do list left over from your first week, and you'll feel a little like a circus performer twirling plates. But there are several activities that are good to start in the second week. They'll take time to complete, too, but you'll be glad you started them now. In fact, there's no reason these couldn't be started in the first week. It's just that the activities listed for the first week are more important to start sooner.

If you're planning to live in Mexico for a long time, or even permanently, you will want to have something other than the FMM tourist card that you received when you crossed the border. That's because the FMM is only good for a maximum of 180 days. Before it expires, you will have to cross the border again with your car in order to get a new one, along with a new vehicle permit. That is, unless you upgrade to an **FM-3 visa** instead. That's what most expats at Lakeside do.

Aside from not having to re-cross the border every 180 days, the biggest advantage (there are many other) is that you can then open a bank account in Mexico. Most Mexican banks require an FM-3 visa (or higher, like an FM-2) in order for expats to open an account. If that is something you'd like to do, now is a good time to get started on the process. It only takes a few weeks to accomplish, is fairly simple, and can be done locally. But, there are some income restrictions. See the Index under Visas for more information.

Another activity you will want to start now is to research your **health insurance** options. You will find that health care in Mexico is approximately 1/3 of the cost of similar care north of the border. And yet, even at the reduced costs, a long-term serious illness or injury could still be financially devastating without some form of insurance. There are many options to choose from in Mexico. But be aware that there is usually a two-month coverage waiting period for private health insurance, so you will want to start this process now. And, do make sure that the health insurance you currently have is extended for at least that period of time in order to avoid any coverage gaps. See the Index under Health Insurance for more information.

One last activity you will want to start this week is to research your Mexican **cell phone** options. As you have no doubt determined, using your north of the border cell phone in Mexico long term is expensive. Mexican cell phone services are much less expensive, especially since many do not require long-term contracts. See the Index under Phones, Cell for more information.

Chapter 3

Your Third Week

Like the activities listed in the two previous chapters, the activities listed here can be done at any time, but are less urgent than the ones listed for the previous weeks. And, no doubt, you still have a very full to-do list.

If you bought a 30-day Mexican **car insurance** policy at the border, it will expire next week. So, you will need to buy new car insurance this week – at a better rate. Car insurance takes effect immediately upon signing up for it and paying for it, unlike health insurance, which has acceptance periods and waiting periods. That's why you don't need to get a new policy before this week. Even though you are not required to buy car insurance by Mexican law, you are required to by Jalisco state law, and the consequences of not having it are quite severe. That is because in Mexico, being involved in a car accident is not a "civil" matter, as it is north of the border. It is considered a "criminal" matter because there is property damage and/or injury. As such, you can be jailed and your car can be impounded if you do not have

"Car insurance takes effect immediately upon signing up for it and paying for it, unlike health insurance, which has acceptance periods and waiting periods."

the right protections. **Do not allow your car insurance to lapse.** It should include bail bond and legal expenses, and it is fairly inexpensive. It can also include towing service. It is the best money you can spend here in Mexico.

By this time, your new house is probably in need of cleaning. Do you want to do it yourself? Have you tried to find a sponge mop to wash the floor tiles with? The only mops available Lakeside are the rope type, so cleaning a house full of floor tiles is not a simple matter. Consider the benefits of having a **housekeeper**. If your house doesn't already include a housekeeper, you can hire a woman (it's almost always a woman) to clean your whole house for very little money,

And, if your house doesn't already include a **gardener**, your lawn and garden might need some work, too, by this time. They're inexpensive, too. But don't hire people who knock on your door looking for work, no matter how sorry you are to turn them away. These are people who will have access to your house, so you'll want to be as careful as you can about whom you choose. See the Index under Housekeepers and Gardeners for more information.

Chapter 4

Your Fourth Week

The activities listed in this chapter are dependent upon you having an FM-3 (or higher) visa. Since you probably started that process two weeks ago, it should be ready now, if everything has gone smoothly.

The first of these activities is to do a **vehicle permit** notification to *aduana* (customs) to reflect your new visa status. The notification is not required by law, but you will lose your vehicle deposit if it expires. By law, your car's permit status follows your status. So, when you get an FM-3 visa, you no longer have to take your car across the border to re-apply for a tourist vehicle permit. Even though you don't have an upgraded vehicle permit document, having your FM-3 visa automatically means that your car's permit has been upgraded (extended), too. The only problem is that some local police may try to give you a hard time for not having an upgraded vehicle permit. They may either not know the law very well in this regard, or they may just want to see whether they can extract a *mordita* (a little bite) from an unknowledgeable gringo. See the Index for more about *morditas*. In either case, you will want to get an official letter from *aduanas* that states that your vehicle permit is duly extended.

The closest *aduana* office is in Guadalajara, but there's no need for you to go there. Any Mexican lawyer (it doesn't need to be a *Notario Público*) can get this done for you at very little cost. You will see signs on buildings advertising for *abogados* (Mexican lawyers/advocates) in your town. At Lakeside, almost all of them are very knowledgeable about immigration laws and the special needs of expats. And since this is a fairly straight-forward transaction, any one of them should be fine, as long as they speak enough English that you feel confident. What you will get is an official, hand-stamped letter from *aduana* confirming that your vehicle permit has been extended beyond the original one.

When you have your extended vehicle permit letter, it's time to get **official certified copies** of your important documents. What this means is that you'll have copies of each of the documents that are certified to be as valid as the originals. Then you won't have to risk carrying around your originals, except in the case of your driver's license, of which you must always have the original when you're driving. The cost is very low, and can be done within a half-hour. This requires a *Notario Público,* though. Again, I recommend Notaria 5 to you. That's located in the orange stucco building at 245-D Hidalgo (that's the *carretera* –the main road) in Chapala. It's in the block just west of the main intersection of Hidalgo and Madero streets. They speak English, and are very easy to work with. The phone number is 376-765-2740.

By the way, a *Notaria Pública* is an office, and a *Notario Público* is a lawyer.

The documents you'll want certified to keep in your glove compartment are those that others might want to see when you're away from home. They include your:

- passport (the two pages with your photo and identification information)
- FM-3 or FM-2 card (both sides)
- tourist vehicle permit
- letter from *aduana* certifying that your tourist vehicle permit has been extended.

If you're over 60 years old, there are two discount cards that you're eligible for, now that you have your FM-3 visa. One is called **INAPAM**, and is the Mexican senior discount card. You'll get big savings (up to half off) on bus tickets, museums, airlines, and some restaurants. See the Index under INAPAM for more information. There's also a Jalisco state senior discount card referred to as **DIF**, which has similar savings. See the Index under DIF for more information.

And, with your FM-3 or FM-2 visa, you can now open a Mexican **bank account**, if you want to. Many expats don't have one, instead choosing to retain their home country bank accounts, and using those credit cards at Mexican ATMs. That works just fine, even long term, as long as you don't need to withdraw more money than your daily withdrawal limit allows. In that case, it helps to have more than one credit card. See the Index under Banking for more information about your options.

Part 5

Living at Lake Chapala

This part of the book is meant to be used as an on-going reference.

Living at Lake Chapala, like living in any other part of Mexico, is not like living north of the border. You will quickly be reminded of all the government services that are taken for granted there (water purification, paved roads), and you will also see how rich your life can be without them. Life north of the border is more predictable, more regulated, more automated, more expensive, and more bland. Looking back, it seems to me to be the vanilla version of life.

Life in Mexico, on the other hand, is a continuous adventure. It's colorful and surprising every day. Even for retirees, no two days are alike. There's much more life on the streets, the plazas, and the parks. There are people still riding horseback on the streets here. There are impromptu fruit and food stands everywhere. The children are generally happier than I've seen north of the border, running around in the neighborhoods like we did in the US in the 50s and the 60s. It's a place where people really interact, and real relationships form.

But it's not always perfect here – not even the weather, contrary to what you may have heard or read. The Lake Chapala area's climate is said to be semi-tropical and perennially spring.

It is sunny almost every day, and the average annual temperature is 67.8°F, but that includes night as well as day, and it includes all the seasons. The real temperatures swing quite a bit from that average. For instance, the hottest time of the year is in April, May, and June, when the daytime temperatures reach into the 80s and 90s every day, and the night temperatures are in the mid to upper 60s. It's then that you'll wish you had air conditioning, even though the air is dry. After the rainy season comes in mid-June, bringing rain frequently at night, the daytime temperatures drop to the upper 70s and 80s during the day and the mid 60s at night, but the humidity is higher. The rainy season lasts until around the end of September, when the temperatures and the humidity gradually decrease until December and January, when the daytime temperatures are between the 50's and 70s, and the night temperatures drop to the low 40s. Then you'll wish you had a heater.

Houses here are generally not equipped with either air conditioners or heaters, but most people do have fans and portable heaters for the extremes. All things considered, the climate here is probably as close to perfect as you're likely to find anywhere – especially, as perfect as you're likely to find anywhere you can afford to live.

In almost all other regards, you'll discover that there are challenges here every day – challenges that will stretch you, make you laugh, surprise you, frustrate you, teach you, and ultimately – make you feel alive.

Chapter 1

Legal Basics

This chapter cannot delve into all the legal system differences between Mexico and north of the border, of course, but there are a few legal basics (some surprising) that are very important for all expats to know. That's why this chapter is listed first.

Mexican lawyers are called *abogados*. They can be licensed by individual states, or they can be licensed by Mexico, which means they can practice in all states. Most of them speak English.

A second type of lawyer is called a *Corredor Publico*. This type of lawyer specializes in commerce issues, such as setting up corporations and filing insurance documents. There are very few of these Lakeside. You'll want to look in Guadalajara for one, or simply use a *Notario Público* (the next level up), instead.

A Mexican *Notario Público* is not at all like Notary Publics north of the border. They can be appointed by a Mexican state or by the federal district of Mexico City, or by passing a difficult application and examination process, and many years of apprenticeship. This is a highly regarded position, therefore. *Notarios Públicos* are the only ones authorized to prepare real estate transfer documents, mortgages, and wills.

Living at Lake Chapala: Legal Basics

All vehicle accidents are considered criminal rather than civil events, since property has been damaged and/or people have been hurt.

Mexico's criminal legal system is based upon Napoleonic Code. That is, you are considered guilty until proven innocent. There has to be some reasonable evidence, of course, that you were involved (the police don't just randomly accuse people of damage, and then force them to prove that they didn't do it). What it does mean is that you can be arrested and detained at the scene for being involved in an accident – regardless of whose fault it is. The process of fault determination may take weeks, months, or more, depending on the complexity of the accident. Your car can be impounded, as well. For these reasons, it's good to have a local lawyer (*abogado*) you can call right away to protect you. Here is one.

> *"Mexico's criminal legal system is based upon Napoleonic Code. That is, you are considered guilty until proven innocent."*

Lic. Spencer McMullen
(045) 331-556-0828
Attorney and official court translator

All legal documents must be signed in blue ink exactly as you signed your passport. Copies of all documents should be black and white only. Color copies are suspected be an attempt to forge documents.

Non-Mexicans are prohibited from participating in Mexican politics. You can discuss politics in private or in small groups, but you can't participate in public protests, sign petitions, or support any politician or party. This is a deportable offense.

The defamation laws against libel (written) and slander (oral) in Mexico used to be very strict. A law was passed in 2007, however, that de-criminalizes them. Until then, the news media were constantly being threatened by defamation suits in order to prevent them from writing negative information (even if true). Now there is only the possibility of a fine, and the possibility of a civil suit, if it's a serious enough case, and if a judge chooses to hear it (there are no juries in Mexico).

There are not as many civil suits in Mexico as in the US, for a number of reasons. They're very expensive, there are no punitive damage awards, and the amount of time for the suit to be resolved is long. Informal and out-of-court settlements are the best options in Mexico.

Having unauthorized drugs, weapons, or ammunition in Mexico is extremely serious. Most drugs and weapons offenses carry significant jail terms. It can also take up to a year to have your case heard, during which time you'll be waiting in a Mexican jail, which is not known for comfort.

Chapter 2
The Towns

The Lake Chapala area is made up of small towns and villages – not cities. This is important when considering what you will find there, and what you won't. Although a Walmart store was built here within the last few years, there are no other "big box" stores or malls to speak of. There's no McDonald's, either. Most people consider this a good thing until they want to buy something above and beyond every-day needs, or when a Big Mac attack hits. Then they have to go to Guadalajara. To my mind, that's as it should be, though – and it's not very far away.

Each town has its own character, as you might expect, and even several characters since many of them have the old traditional area of town, and then a slightly built-out area that's a little more modern. Some even have gated communities now, complete with condo fees, that are every bit as modern as north of the border.

All of the towns have a few features in common. They have cobblestones on their streets, except on major roads. They were originally laid during the days of Spanish rule in the 16th century. The cobblestones are not even-sized, manufactured cobblestone bricks or pavers. They're real, uneven, rounded stones – sometimes quite large. They're not easy to walk on, especially for people with balance problems. They are, however, easy and inexpensive to maintain, they keep the traffic from going fast, and they don't really damage cars that have decent shock absorbers and tires. Many places also have speed bumps (*topes*) that reduce speed even further in some busy areas, eliminating the need for a lot of (costly) traffic lights.

Also, you'll notice that many of the houses, especially in the older parts of town, can't be seen because they're surrounded by walls. This is a carryover from the old Spanish haciendas with their beautiful courtyards in the middle of the houses. The outside may look narrow and rustic, but the entire inside of the "block" is a paradise of flowers and patios. The tradition of the walls has been kept up over time because houses with no walls by contrast look more accessible to burglars. And no one wants to stand out as having the most accessible house in the neighborhood. So the custom continues. That changes as new neighborhoods are built, however. In the newer developments, fewer of the houses have security walls, and front lawns are landscaped in order to open up the view.

Another thing most of the towns have in common is a plaza, sometimes with a central gazebo. It's like a town square where people gather in an open area to sit on benches, sometimes listen to speeches, chat with their neighbors, and enjoy a respite in the open air.

There are towns all around Lake Chapala. But the center of the expat community is on the north shore of the lake – from Chapala on the east to Jocotepec on the west. The farther away from the north shore you get at Lake Chapala, the fewer expats there will be, and the less English will be spoken. Some expats do choose to live on the south shore, and love it, after they feel comfortable living in more rustic areas without the support of other expats close by, and after they have learned enough Spanish to communicate well. But, this is a guide for newcomers, so I will only recommend the north shore for the first six months in this area.

In looking at a map of the north shore, you'll see a road running all the way through the towns. This is called the *carretera* (main road). Each town has a different official name for it. In Chapala, it's called Hidalgo. In some parts of San Antonio Tlayacapan, it's called Calle Chula Vista, and in the La Floresta area, it's called both *Boulevard Oriente Jin Xi* (named after a Chinese immigrant) and *Avenida Luis Donaldo Colosio*. And in Ajijic and west of there, it's named either the *Carretera Ote.*, which is short for *Oeste* (west), or *Carretera Pte.,* which is short for *Poniente,* which also means west. But, it's the same road.

The area to the south of this highway is called the lake side or "lower", as in Lower San Antonio. The area to the north is called "upper", as in Upper Ajijic. The upper parts of the towns tend to be a little more expensive because their views are better, and they get better breezes. More expats tend to live there. There are some breezes close to the lake, of course, but they tend to get blocked by the walled houses there. Most new development is built in the upper areas not only for that reason, but also because that's the only direction expansion can go. There is no real advantage in living closer to the lake as there is in most communities north of the border because the lake coastline is mostly undeveloped. Real estate prices are not much higher there, if at all, for that reason. There are no sand beaches, and no grass, except in the parks. There are beautiful palm-tree-lined boardwalks (*malecónes*), however, and quite a few charming restaurants along the coastline in some of the towns.

Ajijic

The epicenter of the expat community is Lower Ajijic (pronounced ah-hee-HEEK) in *El Centro* (downtown). You'll sometimes see it spelled Axixic (pronounced the same way), which is the indigenous spelling. Ajijic is home to the Lake Chapala Society (including the largest English-language library in Mexico), many wonderful hotels and bed-and-breakfast inns, lots of fabulous restaurants, live music of all sorts, and many wonderful art galleries, art shops, and clothing stores. Aside from all these exciting shops and activities are a beautiful, long, palm-lined *malecón,* a large restaurant-lined plaza, and a large Catholic church – San Andrés – which was founded in the 16th century, and rebuilt in the 18th century. Surprisingly, all the shops and restaurants are intermingled with walled-in residences, many of which have live roosters. Zoning laws seem to be non-existent. This is both good and bad. It's an easy walk to everything, and you feel as if you're in the middle of everything. But you also get the noise, the construction sites, the cooking odors, and the nightclub music. And, when the snowbird tourists arrive from October to April, you get the most tourists, too. That means traffic build-ups, and much less available parking.

The streets in *El Centro* Ajijic are narrow, so many of them are one-way and only allow parking on one side of the street. West Ajijic has wider streets and larger houses that are not so close together. But all of Ajijic maintains its old customs and a slow pace of life, and is very popular. Both Lower and Upper Ajijic are somewhat pricey compared to other towns simply because they're the center of everything. In fact, the farther away from Ajijic you go in either direction, the lower the prices will be – real estate prices, rentals, and everything else.

> *"The farther away from Ajijic you go in either direction, the lower the prices will be – real estate prices, rentals, and everything else."*

There are some less rustic, newer *colonias* (neighborhoods) along the edges of Ajijic that you might want to explore. The houses are further apart from each other, there's more grass, and a more north of the border, open feel. Some of them are quite suburban. On the east side near Walmart, there is La Floresta (where you can also rent horses), and there are many new gated and ungated neighborhoods all along the upper edges of Upper Ajijic that you can easily find on a map.

San Antonio Tlayacapan

To the east of Ajijic is the town of San Antonio, as most people refer to it. The streets are more residential, less compacted, and less "artsy" than in Ajijic. As with most of Lower Ajijic, Lower San Antonio has traditional, rustic house styles. And, it has a typical small-town Mexico feel, too. There's a plaza and small mom and pop stores (*tiendas*). There's also a *colonia* in Lower San Antonio called Mirasol, which has more modern houses with lawns. Upper San Antonio has quite a few more modern *colonias*, like Chula Vista (which has a golf course), along the *Libramiento*. The *Libramiento* is a highway (non-toll, or free) that intersects the main *carretera* across from Walmart in San Antonio. The other end of the *Libramiento* merges with Highway 23, which connects Chapala with Guadalajara. The *Libramiento* was built to provide a shortcut to the western towns without going through Chapala.

Chapala

Chapala is the biggest town at Lakeside. The central part of Chapala (*El Centro*) does not have as high a ratio of expats to natives as most of the western towns. It's very traditionally Mexican, with a large church, a big plaza, and a *mercado* (a covered, on-going market area). It also has big parks. These are great places to take your dogs. There are no pet restrictions in the parks. I've even seen horses

Living at Lake Chapala: The Towns

and cows grazing in Cristiania Park. Chapala also has wonderful lakeside features, like a big *malecón* (boardwalk), a large sculpture fountain, and lots of restaurants.

This is where Guadalajarans come for weekend get-aways, so there's quite a bit of additional traffic in *El Centro* Chapala then, as well as on festival days (which are often). Then there's *banda* music, mariachi bands, fireworks, and parties. So, this is where the non-expat action is. The houses and neighborhoods are traditionally Mexican, too, and get increasingly modern at the perimeters where the newer developments are.

There are a few suburbs to the north, like Chapala Heights, and to the east, like Vista del Lago, too.

Everything costs less in Chapala than in the western towns because it's priced more for Mexicans than for expats. So, unless proximity to particular stores is a high priority for you, you'll stretch your pesos further by shopping in Chapala for everything, including housing. There are more small towns east of Chapala on the north shore of the lake, but I don't recommend them for newcomers because there's not as much expat support there, including the use of English.

> *"Everything costs less in Chapala than in the western towns because it's priced more for Mexicans than for expats."*

San Juan Cosalá

There are lots of small subdivisions along the *carretera* west of Ajijic. They're quite often of mixed character – traditional and modern (more traditional on the lake side). The next sizable town to the west is San Juan Cosalá, which, right along the *carretera*, is very traditional. Whereas most of the other towns and neighborhoods along the lakeshore are a little set back from the *carretera*, in San Juan Cosalá, you will see a great deal of life there because there are houses and small stores, and people milling around. It's fascinating to drive through, and even more fascinating to live there, I should think.

Just before you get to the residential area, there's a stretch of tourist restaurants all along the highway overlooking the lake, which has a tendency of slowing the flow of traffic at times, but it's interesting, nevertheless, as men frantically flag down prospective customers to the parking areas.

The biggest modern development in Upper San Juan Cosalá is the Raquet Club, which has a high percentage of expats, and has its own sports club and beautiful views of the mountains and the lake.

Jocotepec

As you drive west of San Juan Cosalá, you'll notice that there's a fork that goes north to connect to Highway 15, which runs north (to Guadalajara) and south (around the lake). But the main *carretera* dips south through Jocotepec, the western-most town on the north shore of

Lake Chapala. This is one of the oldest towns in the area, having been found by the Spanish in 1528. It has a sizeable *El Centro* area, and a beautiful *malecón* (boardwalk). It's about the size of Ajijic, but it has fewer expats, so far. Most of the town has a very traditional character, with newer developments being built around the edges. The cost of living there is about the same as in Chapala – prices reflect a Mexican, rather than an expat, budget.

Municipalities

All the towns mentioned above fall within two municipalities (counties), which control the various governmental agencies (fire department, police department). The municipality of Chapala includes all the towns and villages east of San Juan Cosalá (including Ajijic). The municipality of Jocotepec includes San Juan Cosalá, and all the towns and villages west. It is much more Mexican in flavor, generally, and housing is much cheaper.

Chapter 3
Language and Social Customs

Some guidebooks will tell you that you don't need to speak Spanish to live at Lakeside because everyone understands and speaks at least a little English because of all the expats. The first part of that sentence is correct: you don't have to be able to speak Spanish in order to get along here. But it's not true that most of the Mexicans here speak English, or even understand it. These are small towns filled with small-town people whose culture has deep roots. They're not as cosmopolitan or highly educated as people are in Guadalajara, for instance, where more business is conducted in English. Unless you plan to live completely closed off from your surroundings, you will want to know more about the people you've chosen to live among. And that means learning their language and customs. You will be amazed at how much you will learn about Mexicans and their culture just by picking up a little language.

Language
The way to get along at Lakeside without knowing Spanish is to rely on your rental or real estate agents, the volunteers at the Lake Chapala Society, your fellow expats, and the Mexican people you'll meet who do know English. And when none of them are around, you'll learn to play charades. When I wanted to buy mosquito repellent at Farmácia Guadalajara soon after I arrived, I had to simulate a mosquito flying around and then landing on and biting

my arm. To my chagrin, I learned that the Spanish word for "repellent" is *"repelente"*. So, it can be done, but you'll probably feel foolish and dependent.

Remember when you lived north of the border, and people got frustrated with those who spoke the wrong language? Now that's you. You're holding up the checkout line because you don't understand what the cashier is saying, you can't telephone customer service for your TV service outage because no one there speaks English, you can't read the words on food or product containers, and you wouldn't know what to say if you had to call the fire department. So, what to do? Below are some activities to begin as soon as possible.

> *"Remember when you lived north of the border, and people got frustrated with those who spoke the wrong language? Now that's you."*

If you haven't already done so, the first activity is to learn to count in Spanish, including all the hundreds, as mentioned in Part 2 (Before Your Move). You'll need to be able to understand and to say numbers for everything you spend money on – which will be a lot when you first arrive. You can learn Spanish numbers using the video at: http://video.about.com/spanish/How-to-Count-in-Spanish.htm. Make flash cards and test yourself until you're sure you know them. And, make sure you can identify them as they're being spoken. Mexicans tend speak quickly. Not only will you need to know your numbers, you will need to be able to identify and count money. So, as soon as you get some Mexican pesos, take some time to study all the bills and coins so you're confident you can identify them when you're in a store under a little pressure. You'll be thankful you put in the study time because paying money and getting change will constitute the majority of your conversations with Mexicans at first.

The second activity, which you should do before leaving your home country, actually, is to buy a new or used copy of "Langenscheidt Pocket Dictionary Spanish". It's a 4" by 6" by 1-1/4" handy Spanish to English/English to Spanish dictionary that you'll love having around. It has a yellow plasticized cover, so it will wear well, and it's small enough to fit into your purse or pocket. It comes in very handy in a pinch.

The third activity you can do before leaving your home country is to install some language translation applications on your smartphone or tablet, if you have one. The first app is **Google Translate**, and it's free. It translates words between any two of 64 languages. You can either type the word or speak it, and it will pronounce the word for you, too. It's very handy. But it does require an internet connection – either 3G or 4G if you're out in the open, or a wireless LAN if you're in a wi-fi hotspot. Another great application is **Word Lens**, and it's $9.99 for each set of two languages. It has two different functionalities. If you hold up your device's camera lens to a sign or document, it will translate the words on it in real time. It's quite amazing to see. The second functionality is a straightforward word translation, whereby you type in a word, and it will give you all the different meanings. Word Lens does not require an internet connection, so you can use it anywhere. The only downside is that it seems to have fewer words in its memory than Google Translate. But it's well worth the price. I've used it for menus, signs at the park, contracts, and my Mexican cell phone instruction manual.

Soon, you're going to want to actually speak Spanish, though. I was intimidated by the language at first. When I was in the United States, I heard Spanish fleetingly on Spanish TV channels, and I thought it sounded like machine-gun fire. The rapid delivery and the rhythm of the language made me think it was almost impenetrable. But as soon as I started recognizing a few words, the mysteries of the language started to reveal themselves. I have three recommendations for you, all of which can be done simultaneously, if you have the time and energy.

Learning a new language does take time and effort – probably more than you anticipate. If you're not studying it an hour a day, the new language just won't sink in and stay there. That's been my experience. So, it's a commitment – one that you probably won't have adequate time and attention for until you begin your second month at Lakeside. Your first month will be hectic enough. But you can certainly get ready and plan for these activities now.

The first activity is to sign up for the next Spanish 1A class at the Lake Chapala Society. It costs 600 pesos (about $50) plus a workbook and a sets of flashcards. The course is 7 weeks long with a two week break, and then you start the next course (1B). You'll be speaking some useable sentences within just a few weeks, and you'll gain confidence as you go. You'll be in a class twice a week for 1-1/2 hours each, with a bilingual instructor and up to 11 other students (usually less). It's a great way to get started, and to feel the support of your class, who will be struggling along with you. It's a very non-threatening atmosphere, but you do have to work in class and at home. It isn't easy, but it is worthwhile.

The second activity is to buy the Rosetta Stone Latin America Spanish language course on computer CDs. It comes in five levels, one building upon the one before. You might as well get all five right away so you have them. The set is sold in many places north of the border for hundreds of dollars. But, if you wait until you're here at Lakeside, you can get a bootlegged set at the Wednesday Ajijic weekly open-air flea market (*tianguis*) for about $30 (See the Index under *Tianguis* for more information). Just find the guy named Taylor, and he'll make you a full set right on the spot. He's located on Guadalupe Victoria street, just to the east of Revolución – but only on Wednesdays, of course.

The Rosetta Stone CD set is very effective, and I highly recommend it. The beauty of it is that it's self-paced. But, make no mistake, it's work and it takes time. Taylor has many other software titles, as well, by the way: Windows Office versions, PhotoShop – lots of software for both PCs and Macs at very low (bootlegged) prices.

I'm not necessarily advocating piracy, but there's a great deal of it here in all forms. Most people take advantage of it, others do not. The choice is yours, of course.

The third activity, if the above two are not enough for you, is to hire a bilingual tutor. Each one has his or her own method of teaching. Some are conversational only, and some use books as well as conversation. Some have small group sessions, and some have one-on-one sessions. You will need to research these on your own, since much depends on your preferences, personality, and budget. Word of mouth references are best, of course, so you'll want to inquire at the information booth at the Lake Chapala Society, and check their bulletin board for tutoring services. Ask other expats you meet, too. The teacher of the Lake Chapala Society Spanish classes will probably also have references. Local newspapers have tutorial services advertised, too (See the Index under Recommended reading. And, you can always askclu for current tutor references on local online web boards (See the Index under Web Boards).

Social Customs
One of the best ways to be accepted by your new Mexican community is to participate in their social customs.

For instance, meeting other adults, even just passing a stranger on a sidewalk, calls for a respectful acknowledgement and greeting. Always wish them *"Buenos dias"* if it's before noon, *"Buenas tardes"* if it's between noon and 7pm, and *"Buenas noches"* if it's after 7pm – regardless of when it gets dark. You'll always get a smile and a similar return greeting. For children, a more casual *"Holá"* (oh-LA) will usually do. Upon leaving, a simple *"Adiós"* is fine, which will be responded to with either *"Adiós"* or *"Que le vaya bien"*, which, roughly translated, means "May it go well with you".

When someone sneezes, you'll want to say *"Salud"* instead of "bless you". It means "health".

When you need to pass or get by someone, the correct expression is, *"con permiso, por favor"*. That means, "with your permission, please". You are asking for their space. They will reply, *"pase"*, meaning "pass", or *"propio"*, meaning "you own it." They have given up their space. If you accidentally bump into someone, you should say, *"perdón"* ("pardon"). If you need someone's attention, you should say *"disculpe"* ("excuse me"). In English, we usually say "pardon" in all three cases, but in Mexico, there's a distinction.

Also, unlike north of the border, you need to excuse yourself if you leave a group, just as you would excuse yourself when leaving a meal. You shouldn't just turn and leave. You should say, *"Con permiso, por favor."*

These may seem like minor courtesies, but they're very important to Mexicans, and they show that you're well bred.

Speaking of space, I have read somewhere that Mexicans' need for personal space is much smaller, so they end up standing closer to us northerners than we are comfortable with. I have not found that to be the case. It seems to me to be exactly the same.

I had also heard that women should never make direct eye contact with, or smile at, Mexican men they don't know – that it's interpreted as being inviting. I have not found that to be the case, either. That may have something to do with my age, but I don't think so. I have found Mexican men to be unfailingly polite and respectful.

> *"Your waiter will never give you the check until you ask for it."*

Another courtesy many Mexicans observe is to wish other diners *"Buen provecho"* ("I hope you get the most from your meal") when leaving a restaurant. The diners will look up and say, *"Gracias"*. Saying it just once (not to every diner) is fine.

Another custom in restaurants is that your waiter will never give you the check until you ask for it. It's considered rude, as if it would imply that you should pay and leave now. The correct way to ask for the check is, "*La cuenta, por favor*".

One other note is that when you want to get a waiter's attention, never call out "waiter". It's considered impolite to be hailed by your profession, just as it would be if you were to call out "cleaning lady". Use "*disculpe*" or "*señor*" or "*señorita*", instead.

Also, to Mexicans, it's considered poor form to suggest going "Dutch" – each paying for his own meal. It's considered an honor, and it will most likely be reciprocated at another time. However, if the tab is agreed to be split, it's always split evenly – even if one person just has a drink, and another has a seven course meal. To be clear, this is true for Mexican culture, but between expats, whatever is agreed upon is fine. Waiters know that foreigners sometimes only pay for their own meals.

> *"Whoever made the invitation to dine should pick up the whole tab, especially if it's a gathering."*

And lastly, regarding tipping, 10% to 15% in restaurants is fine. 20% is going overboard. Don't be tempted to buy respect by over-tipping. Mexicans view tips as tokens of courtesy only, not as pay-offs.

Negotiating Prices

First, there are certain places where negotiating is acceptable, and places where it isn't. For restaurants and grocery stores and for daily staples, no. But for general merchandise, such as clothes and furniture and art purchased from individuals or thrift stores, or anywhere out in the open, yes. For housing (even rentals), sometimes. For cars and large-ticket items, yes. For services, like construction quotes, yes.

But, approach negotiating carefully and respectfully, even if you suspect that the price you've been quoted is a *"gringo"* price (higher than normal because you can probably afford it). Negotiation is a subtle art, one that Mexicans are good at with each other, since they've had lots of practice. Expats, to over-generalize, tend to be ham-handed. The Donald Trump approach won't work here. Don't start your bid at less than half the original

> *"I've heard from Mexicans that some expats start off by offering a price that is so low as to be offensive. Mexicans will often simply refuse to negotiate after that because you've dishonored them."*

price. You'll have better success by starting at a discount of 30%. Offer a reasonable price. It isn't a contest.

Negotiating is sometimes best accomplished by having a Mexican person negotiate on your behalf, as an expat I know does. He has a Mexican housekeeper whom he sends out to buy things for him. She gets the "Mexican" prices, and is good at getting the lowest price possible while still maintaining the honor of the seller. You may not have a Mexican personal shopper since you're a newcomer, of course. But it's an interesting idea to keep in mind.

Chapter 4

Getting Around

There are many options for getting around on the north shore of Lake Chapala. The towns were established centuries ago when people either walked or rode a horse or a mule. So the streets, especially in the centers of the towns, are narrow, and the blocks aren't long. Although some Mexicans still ride horses through the streets, walking is the best way to see each town, to see life as it's really lived. Although the streets are cobblestoned, the sidewalks are level, for the most part.

What requires some extra thought is traveling between the towns. The most obvious solution is to drive your own car. But it isn't the only solution because many people don't own cars here, and many like it that way.

Rental Cars

During your initial exploratory trip to the area, you will want to consider renting a car (*coche*) so you can explore the different towns and neighborhoods efficiently. Later, if you don't have your own car, visiting guests might like to drive around to different areas, too. There are two car rental agencies in the area that I'm aware of that have good reputations (I'm sure there are others, too). One is Hertz Rental, and it's located on the north side of the *carretera* in Ajijic, right next to the post office between Juárez and Aquiles Serdán streets. The other one is Línea Profesional, and it's located between Madero and Guerra streets on the north side of the Carretera in Ajijic. For more information, here is their website: http://tinyurl.com/9nwk5wg. It pays to make reservations in advance because they have a smaller inventory of cars than at thr airport, for instance, and because the days and hours they're open may not be consistent.

> *"Many people will reserve a rental car online, and arrive to find that the rental price they thought they got was only a part of the cost."*

You'll want to be very careful about costs. Many people will reserve a rental car online, and arrive to find that the rental price they thought they got was only a part of the cost. Be sure to ask about the insurance cost up front. There will probably be a **mandatory** daily insurance cost. Often this insurance is tiered. For example, they will tell you that they will require a $10,000 USD hold on your credit card for, say, a $20 USD extra daily payment, but to bring that deposit down to a (more realistic) $1,200 hold deposit, it will cost you something like $50 extra per day. The actual car rental cost itself is very inexpensive – between $14 and $20 per day – but most people mistakenly think this is all they have to pay. The annual cost of car insurance in Mexico may be cheap, but daily, weekly, even monthly car insurance is very expensive.

Taxis

Taxi drivers in this area usually know at least a little English. Many have spent time in the US saving enough money to buy into the market here so they can have a career to support their families, and to be with them. There are taxi stands where you'll see the yellow taxis waiting for fares. These are in the major tourist areas, such as at the big plazas, and they're called "*sitios*" (on site). The *sitios* are preferable to the free-lancers (who don't have "*sitio*" printed on the cars) since *sitios* are licensed by the government.

You'll find taxis to be inexpensive by north of the border standards – so much so that some people use taxis (and buses) instead of having cars. They say that the cost per month is about the same – without the hassle of having to buy or sell a car, or of having breakdowns and repair bills, or of having to get licenses and permits. If you need taxi services after 5pm, though, it's best to make prior arrangements, since their normal hours are during daylight.

Do ask for a rate quote before you begin your trip so there'll be no last minute surprises. And do tip your driver 10% – 15% of the fare. The phone numbers for the main *sitios* in the area are listed in the Appendix. You can also search the area's web boards (also listed in the Appendix) for recommendations of particular drivers.

Hiring a Driver

There are people in this area, usually men, who are hired as personal drivers, either part time or full time. They're usually taxi drivers, so this arrangement is generally just a matter of finding a taxi driver you like and trust, and negotiating your requirements. Some people hire drivers to go to the US border, for instance, or to go to the airport or to go shopping in Guadalajara, or to be a tour guide there for the day. Others pay just to have someone available to drive at any time or for appointments.

Local Buses

The local bus system is very reliable, low-cost, and safe. Most of the Mexican locals who do not have cars use buses to go everywhere. There are full-size buses that travel the length of the *carretera* from Jocotepec to Chapala every 20 to 30 minutes. They start at about 6am and go until about 9:30pm. Some may start a little earlier or run until a little later, and on weekends and holidays, the schedule is less precise. But, be aware that some of them bypass Chapala going east, taking the *Libramiento* shortcut to Guadalajara, instead. So, if your destination is Chapala, you'll want to make sure that the sign at the front of the bus says Chapala – or ask the driver if he or she goes to Chapala.

There are also smaller buses that are about ¾ the size of full-sized ones. These also run along the *carretera* from Chapala. But these buses loop through the side streets of two of the towns – San Antonio and Ajijic. And they don't go further west than Ajijic. You'll want to refer to the

Mexico Travelers Map Guide for the exact routes, or just ride one for the complete loop to see how close it gets to where you want to go. They usually run between 7am and 8:30pm at 15 minute intervals. One senior has told me that she likes these smaller

> *"If you have a DIF senior discount card (see the Index for DIF cards), your fare will be cut in half."*

buses better because the straps and handles for holding on are better. This could be important if you have balance problems because some of the drivers are quite adventurous regarding speed going around corners.

The fares for buses depend on where you're getting on and where you're getting off, of course, but in general, the fare is around 10 pesos. Only cash is accepted, so do bring coins for change or small bills. If you have a DIF senior discount card (see the Index for DIF cards), your fare will be cut in half. When you get on, tell the driver where you're going – the town and the street or landmark, if possible, and he'll tell you what the fare is. When you want to get off, push the red button on the pole near the back of the bus for the bus stop. Or, go to the front of the bus, and indicate to the driver when you want to get off.

Bus stops are not always marked. The places where there are covered benches are a good bet, though, as are places where others are waiting. In general, though, bus drivers will pick you up if you flag them down anywhere along their route – especially near a local attraction or corner.

Tours

During the first few months of your stay at Lake Chapala, you'll probably be too busy to go on any extended travel tours. If you do want to take a tour out of the area, though, you'll be pleased to know that the big tour buses (sometimes called first-class buses) are excellent. They're ideal for long-distance travel, being outfitted with air-conditioning, bathrooms, foot rests, very cushy seating, and sometimes even TVs and videos. They also have bins for luggage above the seats, as well as in the bottom cargo area. Some of these buses run through the Lakeside area into Guadalajara. Those have higher fares, and can be paid for right on the buses.

For real tours, though, you have some other options. The Lake Chapala Society sponsors day tours to various popular shopping locations, like Guadalajara's Galeria Mall, Tonalá, and Tlaquepaque for 200 pesos round trip. The *Cruz Roja* (Red Cross) also has tours, which you can also find out about at the Lake Chapala Society.

One of the most popular tour and travel agencies is Charter Club Tours in Ajijic. Its website is here: www.charterclubtours.com.mx/tours.html. It has a great selection of day trips as well as beach trips, and trips to other popular Mexican destinations (including the US border) on first-class buses. It's located in central Ajijic on the *carretera* in the Plaza Montaña just east of *Calle Colon*.

There are other travel agencies throughout the area, as well. And there are other individual tour operators, too, that have very good reputations, but that are less advertised. The best place to ask about these is at the Lake Chapala Society information booth.

Driving Your Own Car

You'll find that, in general, driving at Lakeside is very similar to driving north of the border.

- Driving is on the right side of the street.
- Street lights are the same colors of green, amber, and red, and they mean the same things. The same goes for turning arrows.
- Handicapped parking is similarly marked.
- Signs are shaped and colored similarly. For example, stop signs are red and have 8 sides. The lettering just says "*Alto*" instead of "Stop".
- Road stripes are yellow and white – the same as north of the border.
- Parking is not allowed along curbs that are painted yellow.
- You're not allowed to block driveways. Most people will have a sign saying "*No Estacionarse*" ("No Parking") on their garage door. Other times, you'll just see a red circle with a capital E and a cross line through it. Sometimes it'll also say "*Se*

usar grua" (a tow truck will be used). If you disobey, your car could be towed by the police at your expense.
- You must wear seat belts.
- The use of cell phones while driving is prohibited, unless you are using hands-free equipment.
- Most people turn right on a red light after stopping.
- Turn signals are used similarly, except that on highways, big trucks ahead of you might give you a left turn signal when it's OK for you to pass them.

Driving is a little trickier, though, for a number of reasons. Speed is measured in kilometers per hour, so be sure to look for that indication (usually in red numbers) on your dashboard's speedometer. And, many of the streets, especially in the older parts of the towns, are very narrow, and they are one-ways. If someone has not parked right up to the curb on the left side, your rear-view mirror on the right side is in danger of grazing a telephone pole.

Similarly, when huge water trucks come lumbering toward you, there may be no other choice than to back up to the last intersection to allow it to pass. Water trucks and other delivery trucks also sometimes double park for a little while, holding up traffic. The cobblestones and speed bumps (*topes*), fortunately, keep traffic from speeding too much, although they do generate a lot of complaints.

In some of the older parts of the towns, there are street dogs who usually know when not to enter a street – but not always. And, children tend to play in the streets more than they do north of the border, so it's important to stay very alert. It helps a great deal to have consulted a map beforehand, so you know which streets are one-ways and more likely to be narrow.

Be aware that there's a rule that's different from north of the border. That is that you must turn on your car's blinking hazard lights when you back up. They'll test you on this when you do your Mexican driver's license road test.

> *"You must turn on your car's blinking hazard lights when you back up around a corner. They'll test you on this when you do your Mexican driver's license road test."*

Keep a special lookout for bicycles. Traffic laws do not pertain to them as they do north of the border, so they can be reckless with impunity.

Most people prefer not to drive at night not only because of the narrow streets but because there's a greater chance that pets and livestock may wander into the streets when there's not much traffic. Animals are not always fenced in.

You need **registration plates** on the car in order to drive legally in Mexico, but they don't need to be Mexican plates. In the state of Jalisco, it's OK if your foreign plates have expired. The status of your Mexican vehicle permit is what matters. That's the document that came with the vehicle permit sticker on the inside of your windshield that you received when crossing the border. Remember that the original vehicle permit that you got is only good for up to 180 days unless you have upgraded your status to an FM-3 or an FM-2 visa in the mean time. Always keep a copy of the vehicle permit document, or better yet – a certified copy of it, in your glove compartment. Don't put the original there, though. A certified copy can be made at a *Notaria Pública* office (See the Index under *Notaria Pública*).

You also need a **driver's license**. It can be from another country, but it cannot have expired. See the Index for more information about how to get a Mexican driver's license, if you cannot renew your foreign one online or by mail.

Under Jalisco law, if your car has been in the state longer than 6 months, then it must comply with the state traffic law, which includes requirements for vehicles, such as having a current **smog check sticker.** This has to be done yearly on or before the month that corresponds to the last digit of your license plate, as follows.

Ending Plate Digit
1 – January   6 – July
2 – February   7 – August
3 – March   8 – September
4 – April   9 – October
5 – May   0 – November

If you have foreign plates with no numbers, just get a new sticker in January of each year. Although the fine for not having a valid sticker is about $100 USD, that fine is completely waived if you get the sticker within 15 days.

Various car repair shops at Lakeside can perform the smog check. To make sure you don't over-pay for this, be aware that the law says that the maximum a shop can charge for gas vehicles is 4 times the minimum daily wage (which currently comes to a total of $242 pesos), or up to 5 times the minimum daily wage for diesel vehicles ($303 pesos).

All **gasoline** stations in Mexico are owned by the government. They have green signs saying "PEMEX", and they are well-run, clean, and efficient. They sell two grades of gasoline (87 octane, and 92 octane), plus diesel. The regular grade sells for around 9.5 pesos per liter (around $3.25 USD per gallon) as of this printing, which is a government subsidized rate. They take credit cards as well as cash. The stations are "full service". That is, someone will come and pump the gas for you. If the attendant also washes the windshield, a tip of 2 to 5 pesos is customary. The one in Ajijic on the *carretera* (between Madero and Juan Alvarez streets) is open every day from 6am to 10pm or so.

Accidents

There's a saying that the first thing you should do if you're involved in a car accident in Mexico that is your fault is to drive away. But, of course, I don't recommend that. Your insurance company won't pay the claim when you get caught (and you probably will, with a foreign plated car), they'll drop your policy, and you'll be in trouble with the police.

If there are any injuries, call **Cruz Roja** (Red Cross) for an ambulance. They're headquartered in Chapala, and their number is **065** or 376-765-2308. They used to be the only ambulance company allowed by law to serve accident victims, but that is no longer the case. So, if a different ambulance arrives, you can use it, too.

If the accident is minor, try to work out a financial agreement with the other driver. That means there won't be a police report, which means the insurance companies won't pay. But, the cost to fix the damages may be less than your deductible.

"Until the agent arrives and takes financial responsibility (which is what you have them for), the police considers you uninsured even if you have your insurance policy with you."

> *"If the police determine that you were under the influence of alcohol or drugs, the insurance company will not represent you, or pay for the claim. They'll also cancel your policy."*

If you plan to call the police and/or your insurance agent, don't move either car, even if the cars obstruct traffic. If the police get involved, call your insurance company immediately, and get an agent to the scene of the accident quickly. Until the agent arrives and takes financial responsibility (which is what you have them for), the police considers you uninsured, even if you have your insurance policy with you. If the accident involves an injury, or if there's major damage to the vehicles or to other property, the police can place you under arrest and impound your car if they determine it was your fault.

That's because vehicle accidents are considered criminal events. And that's why you need to make sure your car insurance never lapses, and that it covers bail bonds and legal expenses.

Everything hinges on the insurance agent showing up to take over. And if you get arrested or they threaten to impound you car, call your lawyer, too. Both your insurance agent's and your lawyer's cell phone numbers should be in your cell phone, and on the Vehicle Accident

Form located in the Appendix. You'll want to make sure you have a copy of it in your car.

If the police determine that you were under the influence of alcohol or drugs, the insurance company will not represent you, or pay for the claim. They'll also cancel your policy.

If you find yourself in a legal bind, you can call the following lawyer.

Lic. Spencer McMullen
(045) 331-556-0828
Attorney and official court translator

Car Repairs

There are many places to get your car repaired Lakeside, from individual mechanics to larger repair facilities. Most of them are in the Riberas del Pilar *colonia*, in Chapala, and in Jocotepec (lower rent areas). Most of them are very good, taking pride in being able to fix most problems. You will find that the labor cost is much lower than north of the border, but the replacement parts may be higher if they're imported. Many parts (and cars, too) are now made in Mexico, so that may not be an issue, especially if you have a common type of car. Astin-Martins and Renaults may be a little more problematic. Most places love to work on Chevys, Fords, Toyotas, and Nissans (which are made in Mexico) because the parts are widely available, and because fixing them is fairly straight-forward.

The smaller shops tend to specialize in such areas as automatic transmissions, mufflers and tailpipes, or suspension and wheel work. Sometimes they're the best at that specialty, but sometimes they're not. The wisest course is to find a good general-purpose shop or individual that has had experience with your type of car, and whom you trust. If they can't fix it, they know who can. They have their own network of trusted specialists – sometimes in Guadalajara.

How to find such a general-purpose shop? It's not necessarily the biggest shop on the *carretera*. It's often the individual genius mechanic working under his carport. Word of mouth recommendations are best. And at Lakeside for a newcomer, that means using online web boards and searching for keywords, such as "repair". See the Appendix for local web boards.

Car Insurance

Not all Mexican car insurance carriers will cover non-Mexicans or non-Mexican-plated vehicles. Your best option, at least at first, is to visit a brokerage that is popular with other expats, and that can write coverage through at least several insurance companies. You'll have a better chance of getting the right policy for your vehicle and your needs. Vehicle insurance is less expensive in Mexico than north of the border.

By the way, many people who have an all-terrain vehicle, golf cart, scooter, or motorcycle, don't think they need insurance – or even registration for the vehicle – thinking that their chances of getting stopped is lower, and thinking they can "self-insure" for any damage their vehicle is capable of causing. Or, they license the vehicle just once to get the plates, and then neglect to follow up with renewals or insurance. I've seen quite a few golf carts scooting around the narrow streets of Ajijic without license plates. But if a child were to get knocked over by one coming around a corner, and hit her head on the cobblestones, the medical expenses could be catastrophic, and the driver could easily end up in the pokey. Insurance premiums for these types of vehicles are often just as much as they are for regular cars (possibly because they're easier to steal). That's why people are willing to take the chance. But, even though the risk may be lower, the consequences are still high.

Most expats I have talked with use the following agency for their vehicle insurance. They're a good bet to at least start with. They're located on the *carretera* (it's called *Hidalgo* there) in the Riberas del Pilar *colonia* on the lake side of the street between San Juan and San Lucas streets in a pumpkin-colored building.

Parker Insurance Services
Hidalgo #248
Riberas del Pilar
Chapala
Phone: 376-765-4666, 376-765-4070, or 376-765-5287

The Parker agency also offers health, home, and travel insurance policies. You will be able to find other agencies, too, if you search for "insurance" on local web boards.

Buying or Selling a Vehicle

In Mexico, selling a car or motorcycle with foreign plates, or even giving it away, is prohibited. The only easy ways to get rid of it is to either surrender it to *Hacienda* (the Mexican treasury), or to drive it to the US to sell it.

You could also nationalize it. You would have to sign the title over to a Mexican national whom you trust, have him/her nationalize it (get Mexican plates for it), and then have the title signed back over to you. There's a large fee for this transfer

"To find out if a car is stolen, check this website: http://tinyurl.com/6t46f7h."

(between $2,000 and $3,000 USD), and it's a hassle, but it can be done IF the car meets Mexico's strict emission standards, and IF the first character of the vehicle's VIN number is a number (which means it was made in a NAFTA country), rather than a letter. There are lots of nationalization scams, though, so I don't recommend doing this without a lawyer involved.

Another downside of nationalizing your vehicle is that your insurance premiums will increase, and your coverage will be reduced. So, why would anyone want to nationalize their car? It's because you cannot own a foreign-plated car if you're applying for Mexican citizenship, or for an FM-2 visa that is not a "rentista" (retiree) type.

I highly recommend that you visit a knowledgeable lawyer when buying a car or motorcycle, too. It's possible that there is money owed on it, or that it's stolen. If it's stolen, it will be confiscated when you apply for Mexican license plates. To find out if a car or motorcycle has been stolen, you can check this website: http://tinyurl.com/6t46f7h.
You'll also want to limit your choices to vehicles that have Jalisco plates, since plates from other states may be more difficult to trace.

Again, a lawyer I recommend in this area is:

Spencer McMullen
Intercasa
Hidalgo #230 (the *carretera*)
Chapala
Phone: 376-765-7553

There's only one auto lot at Lakeside that I'm aware of, and that is:

S & S Auto
Hidalgo #101 (the *carretera*)
Riberas del Pilar
Phone: 376-765-4800

It sells both new and used cars, as well as motorcycles and ATVs. All the vehicles there are sold and rented on consignment.

You'll also see groups of cars along the *carretera* that have red fluorescent triangles on their roofs. Those are also for sale – usually by someone waiting there.

I'm also aware that there are individual auto brokers. Those are people to whom you give your vehicle requirements, and they'll find it at a price you want to pay – for a fee. They cast their net further than just Lakeside. I have seen good feedback on at least one such broker in the Lakeside area on the local web boards (see the Appendix).

Aside from these options, you're on your own if you want to negotiate buying a car from an individual, or go to another area to buy a car. Remember that it must be Mexican-plated for you to be able to buy it legally, even as a give-away.

Getting Your Car Out of Impound

If your car has been impounded for any reason, the police must give you the name and address of the impound yard where it's located.

Here are the requirements to have a *foreign-plated* car released.

- You need to pay the ticket, and to bring the paid receipt.

- If you're not the vehicle owner, you need to bring a notarized power of attorney document, showing that you're authorized to claim the vehicle on behalf of the owner.
- You need to bring the vehicle's title or a receipt from the country of origin.
- You need to bring your passport.
- You need to show that you are in the country legally by bringing your FMM tourist document or your FM-3 or FM-2 visa card.
- You need to show that your vehicle is in the country legally by bringing your vehicle permit document. This is the one you received when you crossed border. It should correspond to the window sticker. Or, bring the extended vehicle permit you may have applied for when you received your FM-3 visa.
- Present the original and one copy of all documents.

The requirements to have a *Mexican-plated* car released from impound are the same as for a foreign-plated vehicle, except that you need to bring your car's registration document instead of the vehicle permit document, and the vehicle *factura* (Mexican title).

Chapter 5

Shopping

Lakeside has an interesting mix of store types. That's because the communities here go back for centuries, long before supermarkets and "big box" stores became popular north of the border. Most areas here are not zoned in the way they are north of the border, and many locals here don't have cars, so the little mom-and-pop corner stores and the small specialty stores are what they're used to.

Guadalajara to the north, however, is modernizing fast, with Costcos, Sam's Clubs, Best Buys, Home Depots, Office Depots, and big modern shopping malls being developed in the city and in the suburbs. And, the Lakeside area is more and more becoming a suburb of Guadalajara. So, it's possible that someday, the Lakeside area will become a boutique area with big box stores on the outskirts, complete with McDonalds restaurants.

Those days aren't here yet, thank goodness, so we still have time to enjoy and support the traditional way of buying and selling goods. I, for one, am glad to be here while this way of life still exists. I like to see little old ladies walking around with their bags, carefully picking out the vegetables for the day's main meal like my grandmother did in Europe. I like the impromptu side-of-the-road barbeques. And I like to see the hand-woven rugs and serapes for sale hanging on tree limbs.

Mercados

There's a tradition in Mexico that every town has a central church, a plaza, and a *mercado* – all in close proximity. Those three features combined are considered the heart of a town. This tradition was established long before there were cars, of course, and it enabled people not to have to walk very far for their daily needs. A *mercado* is a street market, or common market, consisting of a group of booths (usually covered) that sells all the basics for every-day living, like food, clothes, and small toys and trinkets. It's usually open every day. The biggest one today is near the Chapala pier. But, not every town follows this pattern. For instance, San Antonio does not currently have a *mercado*, and neither does Ajijic, although they may have existed there at one time.

Supermercados

"Supermercado" translates to "supermarket", and is the name given to the "big box"' stores, like Walmart. It's also used by *mercados* with aspirations.

Tiendas

Tiendas are individual stores with signs on them, like grocery (*abarrotes*) stores. They have the daily basics of food and household supplies for a neighborhood. There are also specialty *tiendas* like stationery stores (*papelarías*), hardware stores (*ferrerías*), and laundries (*lavanderías*).

Tianguis (pronounced tee-ahng'-gees)
These are weekly outdoor flea markets where local farmers and artisans come to sell their wares. They're very popular with expats, providing opportunities to run into each other and chat. There you'll find fruits and vegetables, meats and fish, clothes, shoes, jewelry, all kinds of art (ceramic, beads, carved, paintings, and sculptures), bakery items, flowers, toys, pirated DVDs and CDs, and household utensils. At times, it's a little like a street fair, with roving marimba players, blaring mariachi music from speakers, street dogs, and beggars – all jostling together on cobblestones.

The most widely attended *tianguis* by expats is held on Wednesdays on Revolución street in Ajijic, just south of the *carretera*. It's geared toward expats in that the prices are a little higher, and the produce is the very best. Every mango is perfectly ripe. The weekly Chapala *tianguis* is just as large, but the wares and prices are geared more toward local Mexicans. The produce is more varied as to ripeness and perfection, and the prices are a little lower. You'll notice that the Chapala *tianguis* is more likely to have listed prices. There are other *tianguis*, as well. Some are in other towns, and some are just for niche items, like organically grown produce. The best way to find out about these (their locations sometimes change) is through the Lakeside web boards (see the Appendix).

The *tianguis* merchants only accept cash, so this is where your diligent study of Spanish numbers and money will pay off. You'll want to know how much something costs first, by asking, "Cuánto?" If it's something to eat, you'll also want to know what the unit of measure is. Usually it's per kilo, which is a little over 2 pounds. Do some quick math in your head – divide by ten, and then subtract a little more. For instance, if something costs *ciento cuarenta* pesos (140 pesos), dividing by 10 gives you $14 dollars, and then subtract a little more. In this case, at the current exchange rate, 140 pesos equals about $10.50 dollars. If all else fails, pull out some paper and a pen, and ask them to write down the number of pesos.

> *"The tianguis merchants only accept cash, so this is where your diligent study of Spanish numbers and money will pay off."*

If you're watching your budget carefully, you may want to write down in a notebook what you paid per kilo at that particular booth, and then comparison shop with the other booths. They tend to stay in the same place from week to week. I've found that the Ajijic *tianguis*'s prices are comparable to Walmart's, but the quality of the produce is better at the *tianguis*. So, aside from wanting to patronize the smaller farms rather than Walmart, I buy most of my produce there – or at the Chapala *tianguis*.

You'll find that meat, poultry, fish, and seafood are not necessarily kept on ice. For that reason, you'll want to shop earlier in the day, rather than later, if you need those.

The only negative regarding shopping at a *tianguis* (aside from wobbling on cobblestones) is that the bags get heavy without having a shopping cart. This is where those giant, blue, plastic, IKEA bags that you brought down from north of the border (you did bring them, didn't you?) will come in handy. Take two of them to the *tianguis* so you can hang one from each shoulder. Then you can balance your load as you go. And, do watch your purse and bags carefully. It would be a good place for pickpockets since people are close together and bump into each other, and are preoccupied.

> *"You never have to worry about the water or ice cubes in restaurants Lakeside. They only use purified bottled water."*

If you want to negotiate prices at the *tianguis*, it's fair game for anything other than food staples. That doesn't mean that every merchant is willing to play the game. Some of their prices are firm – especially if other people are listening. Again, offer a fair price, one that the merchant could say yes to. If you go too low, they'll just be offended, and you'll both lose face.

Buying Water

You most likely already know not to drink water directly from a faucet in Mexico. But here is actually one neighborhood at Lakeside, Chula Vista, where it is said that the water is clean enough to drink since it has its own well system. And many people do that. But in all other places, you'll only want to drink purified bottled water, including the water you make ice cubes with. By the way, you never have to worry about the water or ice cubes in restaurants Lakeside. They only use purified bottled water. The street vendors might be a little more risky, though.

You can buy bottled water from a store or from water trucks that cruise through your neighborhood. The advantage of buying water from the trucks is that they will haul in the big 20-liter plastic *garrafóns* to your kitchen for you. They'll even put one in your dispenser for you. The *garrafóns* are the size of the ones used north of the border for water coolers, so they're heavy. And the older you get, the heavier they get.

You'll probably want to limit your choices of *garrafón* water brands to three of them: Ciel (which is purified by Coca-Cola), Santorini (Pepsi), and Bonafont (Group Danone, makers of Evian and Activia). Those are the most trusted brands, using the best means of purification (reverse osmosis), and they are the only ones the *supermercados*, like Walmart and Soriana, carry. And they'll only take back empties for those three brands.

By the way, when you buy a *garrafón* of water, you're paying for the water and a deposit for the bottle itself. If you buy brands other than those top three from a water truck, that's the only place you can turn the empty *garrafóns* back in for a deposit return or exchange. So, if you buy an off-brand, you can only turn it back in or exchange it when that truck comes around again, which means you have to be home at that time, and hope that you recognize the particular tune it plays (like an ice-cream truck). And, I've heard unsubstantiated rumors that the off-brands may not have 100% purified water. For all those reasons, I recommend sticking with the top three brands. If you find yourself stuck with an off-brand empty *garrafón*, you can always place it outside with your garbage. Someone will undoubtedly take it off your hands, and get a few pesos for it at a recycling center.

If you do use the big *garrafóns* of water, you'll need some kind of dispenser. Some people like the kind used north of the border, whereby you turn the *garrafón* upside-down into a plastic or metal or ceramic dispenser with a valve at the bottom. That requires muscles and skills (and probably luck) that I don't have. But if you do, you can buy them at some local *supermercados*, like Walmart and Soriana, or at Costco and Sam's Club (see the "Where to Buy Things" section below for more about these stores). You can buy ceramic ones at ceramic stores, who usually display them outside on the sidewalk or parking lot.

What I use is a metal holder, about waist high, with which I can easily tip the *garrafón* to dispense water. It does still require muscles to carry the *garrafóns* in and out of a shopping cart, in and out of the car, into the house and into the holder. But I can manage for a few more years.

Of course, you can always buy smaller plastic bottles of water at any store. They're easier to maneuver, use, and refrigerate, and there are no deposits. You can buy dispensers for these, too, if you want. I've seen people place a small water dispenser on their bathroom sinks, for instance, to use when brushing their teeth. A pitcher and cup work just as well, of course.

Buying Groceries

It's most convenient to shop at a *supermercado* like Walmart if you need to buy a wide range of items. The local Walmart is at the very east end of Ajijic, just across from where the *carretera* meets the Libramiento. It's similar to Walmarts north of the border, except for having a smaller selection of items in each category. But it does have categories that Walmarts north of the border don't carry, like motorcycles and mattresses.

Another *supermercado* in the area is Soriana. It's located just north of central Chapala on the Madero highway going north to Guadalajara. It's on the east side of the street between Avenida Pepe Guizar and Los Maestros street. Start looking for the tall red Soriana sign on your right as you go north after the PEMEX station on Madero. It's very much like Walmart, but it has more Mexican items. Those two stores know they're competing against each other, so they usually have price comparison signs along their aisles. There's a broad price comparison survey done each month by the "Guadalajara Reporter" newspaper, and, although the prices fluctuate quite a bit, Walmart usually comes out having lower prices overall – but not by enough to matter.

When you drive into shopping parking lots, you will probably be greeted by Mexican men with buckets and towels. They want to wash your car for you for a few pesos while you're shopping. They're very polite, so you can easily turn them down, if you're not interested.

The quality of the produce in both stores can vary widely, depending on the shipment received most recently. Remember that produce is usually sold by the kilogram, which is a little over 2 pounds. Produce should always be sanitized when you get home. This includes everything that has been grown with water, including un-bagged nuts – but not spices. Some people say that you don't need to purify produce that is either going to be peeled (oranges, avocadoes, bananas) or cooked (potatoes, onions). But I do it anyway because these items are going to be in a refrigerator drawer or fruit bowl with other purified foods. And, they may be peeled or sliced on a cutting board where purified foods will also be cut.

I just make it a habit to purify all fruits and vegetables and nuts. It's very simple. I bought a plastic tub (about the size you might wash dishes in), and I put the produce in there, cover it with purified water, and add some drops of disinfectant (soaking in purified water alone won't kill any bacteria). I set my kitchen timer for 20 minutes, take the items out to drain on a towel or paper towels, and then put them away. I disinfect berries separately in a smaller bowl because they're easily bruised and crushed. I also do nuts separately because they're small and hard to get back out of the bowl. When doing berries or nuts, I just dump the contents of the bowl into a strainer.

The most widely used disinfectants are MicroDyn and BacDyn, both of which can be found in the produce sections of the *supermercados*, and both contain the active ingredient ionized silver. Walmart also has its own "Great Values" branded one. These do not affect the taste of the fruits or vegetables or nuts. In a pinch, you can also use a small amount of chlorine bleach as a disinfectant, but that tends to leave a bleachy taste.

> *"Produce should always be sanitized when you get home."*

In the bakery departments, you don't bag your own items as you would north of the border. You take a big, circular, metal tray (like a pizza pan) and tongs from the bakery counter, and then place each item you want on the tray. Then you take the tray back to the bakery counter, and the person there bags it for you, and places price stickers on the bags. That is, unless the items, like cakes, are already packaged and have a price sticker.

In general, you'll see differences in product packaging. There are more bags and fewer boxes, probably for the sake of cost and space. Powdered detergent and cat litter come mostly in bags, for instance, unless you buy a north of the border brand, in which case the price is much higher. Almost everything is priced more for a Mexican grocery budget, which is anywhere from a third to a half of what a grocery budget would be north of the border.

> *"Smaller tiendas usually close at 2pm on Saturdays, and are closed on Sundays."*

One of the big surprises is that eggs are not refrigerated in stores here. And they seem to be fine that way. I refrigerate them right away when I get home, but I have never found any spoiled eggs. You'll find that the local butter is a deeper yellow, and has a deeper flavor, too. For myself, I prefer the more subtle flavor of imported butter, even though it costs more. In either case, you have to look carefully to see whether the butter has salt (*con sal* – with salt) or not (*sin sal* – without salt). The saltless butter is more plentiful in the dairy cases.

There are two other, smaller *supermercados* that expats are drawn to because they carry more north of the border items and brands. One is El Torito, located in Plaza Bugambilias (the Mexican translation of the beautiful bougainvilleas flowering vine), which is on the south side of the *carretera* in Ajijic between Revolución and Juan Alvarez streets. The other is Super Lake, located on the south side of the *carretera* in San Antonio between Independencia and San José streets. The prices in both of these stores seem to be higher than in Walmart and Soriana because many of their products are imported. But if you simply must have Hungry Jack Complete Buttermilk pancake mix, Super Lake is where to get it.

Most of the *supermercados* are open from early morning into the evening every day, as opposed to smaller *mercados* and *tiendas,* which are more likely to only have one shift of workers. Smaller *tiendas* usually close at 2pm on Saturdays, and are closed on Sundays. But, I doubt that even the large supermercados have 3rd shift night workers, the way they do north of the border. You will see big floor-washing machines in operation among the aisles during the day, people sweeping, and items being shelved from pallets all day long.

The check-out lanes are very similar to the ones north of the border. They're almost all computerized. Walmart and Soriana both take credit cards. Soriana will give you up to 1,000 pesos in cash back from your credit card, if you ask. Walmart will only give cash back using credit cards from Bancomer. El Torito takes credit cards, but Super Lake doesn't.

It's still a cash society here in many ways. That's why it's important to know your Mexican numbers and money. The checkout people are mostly honest, but there are a few who know that expats don't always count their change correctly, and take advantage of it by shortchanging them a few pesos here and there. Also, sometimes bar code prices are wrong, so do watch the monitors as items are being scanned. It sometimes also happens that the prices listed on the shelves are wrong. You can certainly question any discrepancies you find. But business is not as efficient here as it is north of the border. There are more unintentional errors, many seemingly routine transactions take more time, and sometimes you'll have to make a few trips back and forth that would not be necessary north of the border. Time and efficiency are not as important in this slower-paced society.

Before you leave a store, give a tip to the person(s) who bagged your groceries. They're not store employees. They "volunteer", and hope for nice tips. Some have families to support, and it's their only job. Five to ten pesos is fine.

When you wheel your cart out to your car, you'll often find the same car wash guys now offering to help you load your groceries into your car, for a small fee. Again, feel free to accept or decline, as you wish.

Wherever you go to shop, or even just walking around in neighborhoods, you're bound to meet with people begging. Some are blind, some are disabled in some other way, and some ask for contributions to various charities. It's up to you how to respond, of course, but it's best to think about how you'd like to respond in advance. For myself, I prefer to contribute to charities directly, rather than through individuals who might be tempted to dip into their cash box to buy lunch every day. The *Cruz Roja* (Red Cross), for instance, can be contributed to through PayPal. Just ask the *Cruz Roja* table at the Lake Chapala Society how to do that.

> *"Give a tip to the person(s) who bagged your groceries. They're not store employees."*

For individuals, you could establish a policy that you'll only give away 30 pesos per day to the disabled, for instance. That way, you'll feel that you're contributing, but that you're setting boundaries. And some people decline in general to give people money on the street. The reasoning is that it contributes to demeaning the beggar, and it contributes to a cycle of dependency. Thanks, in part, to the influx of expats, there are now many local charities with funds to help almost everyone who needs it, and to help them learn new skills – especially children. Another way to contribute, of course, is to volunteer your services at those charities.

Speaking of children, you will see some selling berries during what should be school hours for them. They have been hired out by their parents to brokers, instead of going to school. The brokers set sales quotas for the children, and if they don't meet them, they get punished by the brokers and by their parents. For that reason, many of them are quite aggressive in their pursuit of *gringos*, in particular. This form of child exploitation is against the law in Jalisco, but it is not always enforced. My advice is not to purchase anything from children.

Where To Buy Things

You can find everything you need Lakeside, if you know where to look. You may not be able to find everything you *want* at Lakeside, but I can tell you a few places to look for those things, too.

As I mentioned earlier, the first things you're going to need when you arrive are spare keys, especially if you can be locked out while in an enclosed back or side yard. I recommend a particular locksmith and key store because they do a good job of filing down the metal burs, which can make the difference between the keys working smoothly or not – or not working at all, so you have to go back again to have them re-filed. It's a small, yellow shack on the corner of Revolución and the *carretera* (the main highway) in Ajijic. It's called *Cerrajería Cardenas* (Locksmith Cardenas), and it's located to the east side of the Bugambilias Plaza, right next to Salvador's Restaurant.

Most houses Lakeside are rented or sold as furnished, knowing that it usually isn't cost-effective for expats to bring their own furniture with them. So, you may not need furniture right away. But if you do, or if you'd like to pick up some decorative or art pieces, your best values come from re-sale shops and thrift stores, sometimes called bazaars (or bazars). You'll find many of them all along the *carretera*, and in central Ajijic. Some of these shops carry both used and new items, so they're always fun to browse, whether or not you're looking for anything in particular.

You can also have fun looking at yard sales, which are usually called bazaars (or bazars), too. There are also advertisements listed on bulletin boards at the Lake Chapala Society and at popular expat stores like El Torito, Super Lake, Walmart, and Soriana for items for sale or items wanted. Local periodicals, like the monthly "El Ojo de Lago" magazine, also have classified advertising in the back. New furniture, appliances, ceramics, house decorations, linens, and clothes can also be found at Lakeside just by exploring. But you may find the selection somewhat limited based on what you're used to.

The next places to look are in Guadalajara. There are four places I recommend for you to look next.

1. The first is the *López Mateos* group of "big box" stores. This is the only place beyond Lakeside that I recommend newcomers can drive to alone for shopping. What's there is a big Walmart store, a

Mega store (like Walmart), a Costco, a Sam's Club, and a Home Depot. The Costco and Sam's Club are membership stores, so you'll want to bring your membership card from north of the border with you, or bring your passport as identification if you want to become a member. It costs something like $40 dollars. This is the closest place to buy decent bed linens, by the way, of which there are few Lakeside. The way to get there is to take the Lakeside *carretera* west, and then look for the sign as you approach Jocotepec to take the right cutoff to Guadalajara. This is a rough, as yet unpaved, road that merges onto Highway 54 (Guadalajara-Morelia) going north to Guadalajara. It's also called the Guadalajara-Colima Highway, and as you go north on it, it's also called the Guadalajara-López Mateos Sur (which means South). After about 30 minutes of going north, right after the town and golf course of Santa Anita, you'll see the big stores on the right. You'll probably miss the exit once you realize you're there, so just turn back around.

2. The next place I recommend is the Galeria Mall. The two anchor department stores in the mall are Sears and Liverpool. The Sears store is more upscale than the Sears stores are north of the border. The quality is more like Macy's. And, the Liverpool store is very upscale and expensive – more like Saks Fifth Avenue. And then there are some interesting smaller stores in the mall. If

you're really hungry for McDonalds or Dairy Queen or Krispy Kreme's, they're there, too. Plus, this mall is surrounded by a Walmart, a Mega store, a Costco, and a Best Buy. Most of these places will deliver big items Lakeside for you. The way to get there, at least for the first time, is by taking a tour bus. You can buy your round-trip ticket for 200 pesos at the Lake Chapala Society. The trip is an hour drive in complete luxury each way, and your purchases can be stored underneath the bus in the big cargo areas. You leave at 9 and come back around 4:30.

3. My next recommendation is the town of Tonalá on the east end of Guadalajara. It's a major trading center for Mexican handcrafted gifts and decorative items, such as furniture, blown glass, papier maché, ceramics and more. The prices run from inexpensive to expensive, and everything in between. In fact, many of the handcrafted items you see in stores Lakeside are wholesaled from Tonalá. Visiting Tonalá is part of a 1-day tour offered by the Lake Chapala Society and by Charter Tours and Travel in Ajijic. Both tours combine shopping in the town of Tonalá with shopping in the town of Tlaquepaque on the same day, since the towns are fairly close together.

4. The town of Tlaquepaque is also a trading center of handcrafted items. These tend to be more upscale and gallery-worthy items, like one-of-a-kind art pieces, jewelry, artisan furniture and decorative

items. It's well worth visiting, even if the items may be a little out of your price range. As with most handcrafted items in Mexico, you can try negotiating a price that suits your budget.

There's a store you might want to visit in Guadalajara, if you're a book-lover. That's Sandi Books. It's the largest seller of new English-language books in Guadalajara. It's located close to the López Mateos Highway further north than the "big box" stores – in the Chapalita neighborhood (*colonia*). You can visit their website for more information here: http://www.sandibooks.com.

At Lakeside, you'll see a few used bookstores by driving around, and you'll see books by local authors (including this one) in various places, like the Diane Pearl Colecciónes gift shop in Ajijic and Hotel La Nueva Posada (you can Google these for addresses) and other inns, shops, and restaurants where expats congregate. Aside from that, there's a small bookshop on the west side of Bugambilias Plaza on Juan Alvarez street, named "Book Store". It has just a smattering of books in English, but it also has the Sunday New York Times and north of the border magazines. Plus, it has the local maps I recommend: the fold-out one by Sombrero

"The best place to buy the Rosetta Stone language course is at the Wednesday Ajijic weekly open-air market (tianguis) for about $30."

Books (cartography by Tony Burton), and the Mexico Travelers Map Guide to Lake Chapala, Ajijic and Environs by Mexico Travelers Information.

As I mentioned earlier, the best place to buy the Rosetta Stone language course is at the Wednesday Ajijic weekly open-air market (*tianguis*) for about $30 (See the Index under *Tianguis* for more information). Just find the guy known as Taylor, and he'll make you a full set right on the spot. He's located on Guadalupe Victoria street just to the west of Revolución – but only on Wednesdays, of course. He has many other software titles, as well: Windows Office versions, PhotoShop Elements, games – and lots of software for both PCs and Macs at very low prices.

If you're interested in plants for home and garden, you'll find you're in paradise. Lakeside is lush with plants all year around, and there are many nurseries (*viveros*) here. One of the largest is Flora Exotica, which is located on the northwest corner of the Libramiento and the *carretera*. There's another nice one beside Telecable on the south side of the *carretera* in the Riberas del Pilar neighborhood between San Juan and San Jorge streets. You'll see *viveros* signs all along the *carretera*, in fact. And if you particularly like cacti, many of the *viveros* west of Ajijic specialize in them. Seeds are a little more difficult to come by. The garden center two doors east of 7-Eleven on the corner of the *carretera* and San Mateo in Riberas Del Pilar has a few flower, vegetable, and herb seeds, and so do some hardware stores. But many people also buy them online north of the border, and have them sent. You can check local web boards (see the Appendix) for peoples' online recommendations.

For those who are used to having an Office Depot nearby north of the border, there are none at Lakeside. There are some in Guadalajara near Highway 54, though. You can Google "Office Depot Guadalajara" or "Office Max Guadalajara" for locations. The reason this is significant is that the *supermercados* Lakeside have very few paper and office supplies. What they have are school supplies, basically. There are many stationery stores (*papelarias*) everywhere, but they're not quite what you'd expect – concentrating, again, on school supplies. They do have copiers, fax machines, and sometimes public computers, though. But it would appear that very few locals have need of legal pads, full-size staplers, and the like. You'll need to go to Guadalajara for those, or order them online. They'll deliver. Be aware, though, that if you're looking for pads of paper online, they're not in the "paper" section (as Google translates it), they're in the subsection called "blocks" (which means paper pads) within the "Office" section. Also, file cabinets/drawers are called *archivistas*.

The closest Craigslist for this area is the Guadalajara one. But there don't seem to be many listings for merchandise for sale on it, for some reason. However, many online stores, like eBay and Amazon, do allow purchases from Mexico, for a higher shipping fee, and an approximately 10 day shipping time for regular government mail service.

This is where having a mailing service (see the Index) comes in handy, since vendors don't have to ship internationally.

What You Won't Find

Because most people north of the border work away from their homes, industries there have developed products to support that lifestyle. A prime example is **frozen meals**, like Lean Cuisine™. In contrast, most Mexicans who live in small towns have at least one adult, usually the woman of the house, who does not work outside the home. They're expected to cook. So the need for frozen meals is not as strong as it is north of the border. Also, frozen food requires stores to spend more on electricity for freezers, and electricity is comparatively expensive in Mexico. The result? No Lean Cuisine™ – yet. Some frozen food is starting to appear here, though. There are pizzas, shaped hamburgers, French fries, and a few appetizers, like flautas, in the frozen food sections. And there are lots of bagged cut vegetables as there are north of the border. But not full meals, to speak of. Fortunately for us expats, the *supermercados* do have rotisserie chickens, though, for quick meals. And, Costco and Sam's Club does have some frozen lasagnas and Chinese food that are very good.

> *"No Lean Cuisine™ - yet.*
> *"*

But speed is not what meals are all about here. Meals are still a time for everyone in the family to be together. The main meal of the day is called the *comida*, and it usually lasts from 2pm to 4pm, with multiple courses. Then, families will have a smaller meal in the late evening, around 9pm, called the *cena*. So, **fast food restaurants** haven't arrived here yet, either. You have to go into Guadalajara to find a McDonalds or a Burger King. But Dominos Pizza does have a small restaurant and delivery store here in the little plaza to the west of Walmart on the *carretera*. I stopped in there for lunch one day, hoping for a slice, but they only make whole pizzas, and it would have taken 15 minutes to make. When I did order a full pizza, I found the sauce spicier than north of the border.

When I first arrived, I looked high and low for a **sponge floor mop**. They're not here. Not one. And Swiffer™ mops? Forget about it. People in this area only use the rope-type mops. I presume this is because almost all floors are tile, so the sheer amount of square footage would wear out a sponge mop head or Swiffer cloth fairly quickly, and people may not be able to afford the replacements. Rope mops may be one of the reasons people hire housecleaners, actually. It takes a lot of muscles to twist and squeeze them repeatedly, and few *gringos* want to put in that effort (or maybe it's just me).

There's one other item that eluded me – for a while: **bug repellent containing the chemical DEET**. What I found out was that the acronym DEET is not used here. The entire chemical name is spelled out in the ingredients list, which is: dietil-meta-toluomida. "OFF Family" in an orange aerosol can has it in 15% strength. That's the only brand I've found so far, although there are supposedly two other brands that have it here: Ultrathon and H24. If you want DEET in stronger doses, you'll want to bring some with you, or purchase some through Amazon.com or eBay, and have it shipped

Mexico has a consumer protection agency called PROFECO, if you want to file a complaint. The website is: www.profeco.gob.mx/english.htm. You'll need a lawyer, though, to navigate the paperwork and to represent you. This is a very powerful organization, which has the authority to fine merchants more money than you're owed, making it easier for merchants to give in to your legitimate claims.

Chapter 6

Safety

Had this book been written in 2011, the subject of safety would not have merited its own chapter. But enough has changed in 2012 to cause people both at Lakeside and north of the border to take a second look at the issue of safety in determining whether the Lake Chapala area is a good place for expats to live.

In May of 2012, 18 Lakeside Mexicans were kidnapped, and their mutilated bodies were found a few weeks later a little north of Lakeside. These horrific acts were determined to be drug cartel-related, although none of the victims were known to have been involved in the drug trade.

These were terrorist acts committed 1-1/2 months prior to the national presidential elections held on July 1st. Some political analysts have said these acts were committed in order show that the ruling party was ineffective in the war against drugs, its central theme, and that the cartels are still in control of the country. Others have said that this scenario was inevitable as the major cartels try to claim one of the last remaining undominated areas of Mexico, and that the timing was coincidental.

Whatever the reasons, Lakeside residents, both locals and expats, were stunned. Daily life came to a standstill. The local and state police arrived, as did the military. Many, possibly most, of the perpetrators were caught, and their safe houses and weapons caches were found. To date, no other incidents of this kind have been reported in this area, and the presence of the police and the military has subsided. But there's a new normal at Lakeside, as there is in every community that has been hit by violence or tragedy. Although expats were not targeted in these incidents, everyone grieves for their neighbors and friends. And now everyone knows that no place is exempt from crime, not even the Lake Chapala area.

There were widespread rumors that many expats were going to leave, but no mass exodus has been reported to date. The expats I've spoken with consider Lakeside their home, and plan to stay here to work through whatever time brings. So far, it has brought communities closer together.

It's an unfortunate fact that there are destructive elements in every society, whether it's highly developed or not. Most of the time, these elements aren't noticed by average citizens, like the workings of the Mafia and other pervasive criminal organizations north of the border. They only become apparent when their fault lines rupture. But, after the shaking stops, life begins again, often with a deeper appreciation for life and the community.

Overall, the crime problems at Lakeside are about what you'd expect in any community of this size. The expats generally have more money than the locals do, so it would be hard to imagine that there would not be the occasional house burglary and theft and vandalism. But these do not dominate conversations here.

In fact, there is less fear here on a day-to-day basis than any place I have lived north of the border. There are no roving gangs, and children play unsupervised in their neighborhoods – even into the evenings. I have never seen a woman of any age, local or expat, leered at or been made to feel uncomfortable in any way on the streets. Quite the opposite, in fact.

This is not to say that expats don't need to act prudently. Houses and cars should be locked, money should not be visible, and expensive jewelry should be kept to a minimum. And you should avoid walking alone at night – especially if you've been drinking. That's just common sense in any community.

> *"The chances that you'll be a victim of crime are miniscule."*

In summary: the fear of crime should not be a reason for you to stay away from Lake Chapala. The chances that you'll be a victim of crime are miniscule.

Chapter 7

Medical Care

The primary reason many people consider moving to Mexico is that the cost of living here is lower. A large part of that cost is for health care, for insurance, services, and medications. Aside from costs, quality of care is also a consideration.

Medicare

These considerations require more thought at age 65 for US citizens, in particular, since that's the age when they become eligible for free health services through the government's Medicare program. To date, a Medicare benefit claim is only valid if the service is performed within the US or its territories – with two exceptions. The first exception is if you can prove you are just a tourist in Mexico, and that the service is the result of an emergency. The second exemption is if the hospital from which you get the service (in Mexico or in Canada) is closer than the closest hospital in the US that can treat your medical condition.

> *"A Medicare benefit claim is only valid if the service is performed within the US or its territories."*

There are a few organizations lobbying the US Congress to have Medicare benefits extended to seniors living in

Mexico. The primary one is AMMAC – Americans for Medicare in Mexico – a chartered Mexican non-profit whose website is www.medicareinmexico.org. But, until the day Medicare covers claims from Mexico (if ever), US senior expats will need to decide whether their health needs can be met here. For most expats, the answer will be yes.

Quality of Medical Care

There are very good general practitioner doctors Lakeside, some of whom have graduated from and/or interned at very good US and Canadian medical schools and facilities. Most speak English, and take much more time with their patients than doctors do north of the border. You can count on at least a half hour with the doctor per visit. They're not pressured to go from one patient to the next in as short a time as possible.

There are also labs and clinics here that are well regarded. They may not have the fanciest equipment or high-rent facilities Lakeside, but most of them are competent, caring, and knowledgeable enough to do a good job, and to know when to refer you to a specialist at Lakeside, or to one less than an hour away in Guadalajara, which has world-class medical specialists and hospitals. The Hospital Mexicano-Americano, for instance, has international health certification. And in Mexico City, the ABC Hospital (American British Cowdray Hospital) is also a world-class teaching and research facility, with board certified specialists.

Incidentally, you don't need any referrals to go to a specialist. And, you can just walk into any clinic or lab, and ask for tests of any kind – blood work, urinalysis, whatever you think you need. And you'll get the results to take with you.

> *"You don't need any referrals to go to a specialist. And, you can just walk into any clinic or lab, and ask for tests of any kind."*

The medical community here expects you to be responsible for your own health, and to keep your records yourself – even x-rays. So, when you do go to a doctor, you'll want to bring all the records with you that might be pertinent. To me, this is a refreshing approach, treating patients as adults.

Cost of Medical Care

Most medical services and medications are from 40% to 70% lower than north of the border. For instance, going to a lab and having blood drawn to determine my blood type cost me about $9.00 USD at the Ajijic Clinic on the *carretera*. A visit to a doctor will cost between $35 and $100 USD, and some doctors will make house calls, as well. Doctors frequented by *gringos* usually charge the higher fees, but that doesn't necessarily mean better services.

Why is the cost of medical care here so much lower? Aside from lower wages, there are almost no medical malpractice suits here, so medical malpractice insurance premiums are lower, and there's no need to order redundant or unnecessary tests, either.

Pharmacies

The pharmacy chain most popular with *gringos* Lakeside seems to be Farmácia Guadalajara, which has a number of stores along the *carretera*. They're open 24/7, and they're among the few that will give you an "official *factura*" (invoice/receipt) for your medications. The other one that will give you an official *factura* Lakeside is the Walmart pharmacy. The reason this is important is that an official *factura* is required by insurance companies for reimbursement of medications. If your medications are part of your treatment for a covered accident or illness, you'll want to go to either of those two pharmacies. If not, you can certainly go to any of the "*similares*" pharmacies you'll see at Lakeside. They sell discounted drugs, which are usually generics. These pharmacies keep their costs low by accepting only cash, which not only eliminates credit card fees, it allows them to

"The reason this is important is that an official factura is required by insurance companies for reimbursement of medications."

under-report their sales figures to the government. And that's why they won't give you an official *factura*.

The generic drugs Lakeside are like generic drugs anywhere: they're great if they work for you, but in some cases, they may not have the same effect as branded drugs. But, I'm not aware of any poor quality issues for these generics, so they may be worth a try at a reduced cost.

> *"In Mexico, pharmacists do not need to have the extensive education and licensing required north of the border."*

Branded medications are actually already much less expensive than north of the border. My own medications from Farmácia Guadalajara are 25% of what I would have to pay north of the border (without insurance), and they don't require prescriptions, so you save on doctor's visits, too.

Also, do ask the pharmacy you choose whether they give discounts for DIF or INAPAM discount card holders (see Index for more information on these). Some do, which can save you even more money.

And, lastly, be aware that in Mexico, pharmacists do not need to have the extensive education and licensing required north of the border. This means that you need to make sure your doctor is aware of all the medications you're taking in order to prevent medication conflicts.

Dental Care
Mexico in general is known for being a dental care tourist destination. That is, the quality and costs of care are so good that people plan their vacations in Mexico, in part, to get their teeth fixed or to be fitted for dentures. The Lake Chapala area is no exception. There is an abundance of excellent English-speaking dentists, many of which can easily be found by cruising the *carretera*.

Choosing Your Medical Professionals
Your best choices are usually found by referral. The web boards (see the Appendix) frequently have comments about various doctors and dentists, so those are excellent places to begin your research. Or, you ask your Mexican health insurance agent which doctor(s) the *gringos* go to.

Cruz Roja (Red Cross)
The Cruz Roja in Mexico is a non-profit organization that assists victims of natural disasters and accidents. Cruz Roja ambulances used to be the only ones authorized to assist accident victims, but private ambulance companies are now also authorized. Cruz Roja has their own clinics, to which they drive accident victims for initial stabilization. What makes Cruz Roja services so special is that they are free to those who cannot afford to pay, which makes them a critical community resource for low income locals. For additional information, see their website at

www.cruzrojachapala.com. Their phone number is in the Appendix.

Medical Clinics

There are a number of clinics at Lakeside that are open around the clock for emergencies. They also offer walk-in laboratory and x-ray services, or they have special arrangements with local providers of these services. Aside from the Cruz Roja clinic mentioned above, there is the Maskaras Clinic (which also has ambulance services) on the *carretera* (Hidalgo 79-G) in the Riberas Del Pilar colonia of Chapala. The nearest cross-street is San Jorge. Their website is here: www.maskarasclinic.com. Another clinic is the Ajijic Clinic, which also has an ambulance service, located on the *carretera* in Ajijic at #33. The cross street is Javier Mina. This one is used by many expats, and is run by physicians from Guadalajara.

> *"What makes Cruz Roja services so special is that they are free to those who cannot afford to pay."*

IMSS Insurance

Although the cost of medical services is much lower in Mexico than north of the border, a serious illness or surgery can still be financially devastating. A heart attack could cost $10,000 USD, for instance, for full treatment and stabilization, and hospitals do want to be paid when the patient leaves, in addition to wanting $1,000 USD for admittance.

Some expats self-insure. That is, they feel they have either enough money to pay for full treatment in Mexico, or they feel they have enough money to pay for medical stabilization in Mexico, and then to pay for medical helicopter fare to the US to be covered by Medicare for full recovery. Other expats feel that they are at low risk for health problems, and save a certain amount of money every month toward medical bills rather than pay insurance premiums. For everyone else, some form of medical insurance is a good idea.

One of the basic insurance programs in Mexico comes from the Mexican Institute of Social Security, or IMSS. It has many services and facilities, including running its own outpatient clinics and general hospitals. It's very much like an HMO insurance organization. IMSS also has pharmacy services, but there are many complaints that this is almost a useless benefit since they are poorly stocked, and rarely have the medication needed. And, they don't reimburse expenses from other non-IMSS pharmacies.

All Mexican nationals have to be offered this insurance by their employers. Foreigners who have either an FM-2 or an FM-3 visa are qualified to join. There's usually no medical exam, but not everyone is accepted. Your application to join will include questions about pre-existing health conditions, which may cause some coverage to be excluded. And, coverage is phased in over a period of three years.

There is a waiting period of between 6 to 9 months. The fee is approximately $270 per year for seniors, but applications are only accepted in January and February, and in July and August.

Expats who join IMSS usually do so for the hospital benefits as a fall-back plan. The day clinics get very crowded, so you could easily end up waiting all day in a very noisy waiting room to get treatment. And the doctors and support staff don't always speak English. You'll want to bring a translator. The doctors usually work there part-time, and then have their own practice, as well, so you never know whom you're going to get. But, if this is the only health insurance you can afford, it's better than nothing, and will certainly help in a dire health situation. You can read more about the IMMS here: http://tinyurl.com/8aw8stm. It's best to contact a lawyer (*abogado*) or other facilitator who knows how the system operates with regard to expats. You can also research expats' experiences with IMSS on the local web boards (see the Appendix).

> *"Some expats have both IMSS insurance and their own private insurance, and they pick and choose services and providers based on the individual medical situation."*

When researching whether certain procedures are covered, make sure you find out how much money will actually be paid. It's nice to be covered, but if the payment limit is low, it may not seem like such a good deal. Also, make sure you find out what coverage really means. For instance, does it include a room, food, the surgeon, anesthesiologist, nursing staff, and supplies? Sometimes these line items are not included in treatment quotes, and can make a big difference.

"Hospitals in Mexico generally expect someone to bring food for you."

Seguro Popular Insurance

Another Mexican government health insurance program is called Seguro Popular. Like IMSS it includes clinics, hospitals, and pharmacies. You cannot be a member of Seguro Popular if you have any other insurance, though, including IMSS. In fact, it was established for Mexicans who could not afford IMSS, or were not qualified for it.

The annual fees are calculated on a sliding scale based on income, and both the federal and state governments subsidize the remaining fees. This insurance is generally used by expats for the free and near-free medications. The down-side is that only minor- to medium-level ailments are covered, and that the outpatient clinics are just as crowded and noisy as the IMSS ones. Here is a booklet in Spanish regarding the program coverage: http://tinyurl.com/7fpdtyz.

Private Health Insurance

There are many options in this category, but, generally, private health insurance in Mexico consists of what is referred to as "major medical". That is, it covers only hospitalizations and associated costs. It does not cover routine doctor visits or prescriptions. That's because those are considered inexpensive enough that most expats can afford to pay for them out of their own pockets. Some expats have both the IMSS insurance and their own private insurance, and they pick and choose services and providers based on the individual medical situation.

There are Mexican health insurance companies, and there are international health insurance companies. Most Mexican ones will not write a new policy to a person who is 65 years old or older, and they routinely cancel policies when a person turns 75 or so.

That leaves the large international health care insurance companies, like BUPA, IMG, ING/AXA, and Grupo Inbursa. Rather than spend a great deal of time trying to research which one is best for you, you might as well go to an insurance broker, who can do that for you. Many expats I've talked to use the following broker for their health insurance and their auto insurance.

Parker Insurance Services
Hidalgo #248
Riberas del Pilar
Chapala
Phone: 376-765-4666, 376-765-4070, or 376-765-5287

Private health insurance in Mexico is much less expensive than north of the border, but it is still a significant cost. Someone in their 60s without extensive medical problems can expect to pay about $275 per month (payable annually or semi-annually). Again, that's for major medical coverage only.

Make sure that your insurance coverage extends to all of Mexico, and not just if you get ill locally. You'll also want to consider having coverage for emergency medical helicopter service to the US if you have family there, Medicare, a special clinic, or if you'd just feel more comfortable there. And, of course, you'll want to find out what is included and excluded, and whether the insurance payout is on a percentage basis of the charges, and if there's a maximum payment limit. And again, do check the local web boards.

> *"You'll also want to consider having coverage for emergency medical helicopter service to the US if you have family there, Medicare, a special clinic, or if you'd just feel more comfortable there."*

Chapter 8

Home Life and Services

For most expats, everyday life in Lake Chapala revolves around people, animals, nature, and favorite pastimes like writing, reading, art, exploring, volunteering, and travel. At least, that seems to be the ideal. In order to have the time for these interests, your home life and services need to be reasonably stable. This is an area where you'll find many differences between what you're used to north of the border and here in Mexico. To be candid, Mexico is not known for its efficiency. And you'll be surprised at all the conveniences you took for granted north of the border. It takes more time, more trips, and more patience to get your home technology up and running smoothly, and maintained, unless you live an extremely austere life here (which is not a bad idea, either).

Part of the challenge is the language barrier, but that's not the major part. If you can afford home services like a housekeeper and a gardener, there are schedules to maintain. Figuring out how to use your home phone and cell phone, and how to dial various places can be challenging, too. But, once these are learned and set up, your time will be freed up to enjoy the more satisfying aspects of your new life here in Lake Chapala.

Household Help

You will most likely be able to afford more household help at Lake Chapala than you could have north of the border because wages are much lower here. The minimum wage in the US is $7.25 USD per hour, and the minimum wage in Mexico is 60 pesos per day, or about $.56 USD per hour (assuming an 8-hour day). That's the minimum wage employers must abide by, but not everyone does. There are certainly many rogue businesses that set their own rules, and only report to the government what is most convenient to report.

> *"Hiring Household help is generally considered an informal cash arrangement, one that doesn't need to be reported."*

Domestic employees are a special class of employees, and only require reduced employer obligations. Hiring household help is generally considered an informal cash arrangement, one that doesn't need to be reported. But it does have its own customs and expectations that you will want to abide by as a good member of the community.

1. You only need a verbal understanding to hire household help. However, a written agreement detailing work duties and schedules is a good idea.
2. You're expected to pay only in cash, and on a weekly basis. If the person works several times per

week, the cash should be paid on the last expected work day of the week.
3. You are expected to pay 15 days worth of wages as a Christmas bonus (*aguinaldo*) on or before the 20th of December. This can be pro-rated, if the person has not worked for you for an entire year. To calculate how much is expected, figure out how much the person usually earns per day, and then multiply that times 15. As an example, suppose you've agreed to pay a person 200 pesos per week for services (regardless of how many days they come or hours they work). They're making 29 pesos per day (200 divided by 7). Multiply that times 15 days, and you owe them 435 pesos for *aguinaldo*. If they only worked half of the year for you, you only owe them half that, but it's Christmas, so it's easy to be generous.
4. You're also expected to pay a minimum of 6 days wages, plus 25% of that, after each year the employee has worked for you.
5. You will, of course, want to give as much notice as possible if you intend to discontinue his or her services (without formal cause). You're expected to pay three month's wages severance pay, plus 20 extra days pay for each year he or she has worked for you.

Regarding how much to pay per hour for household help, the locals in Lake Chapala know that many *gringos* wouldn't dream of paying them less than a dollar per hour, so a double standard has evolved. Locals who work for *gringos* ask for more money per hour than they would for a Mexican employer, and, if they come well recommended, they get it. The norm in this area seems to be between 30 to 40 pesos per hour for a housekeeper. It's more for gardeners and handymen because men here make more than women.

If you rent your house, you may have inherited a gardener and/or a housekeeper as part of the lease. In that case, the issue of wages is not a concern for you, and neither is hiring or firing. But that isn't necessarily a positive circumstance. In the case of a housekeeper, if you prefer not to be home when she's there (because you have to keep moving around to keep out of her way), that means that she will have keys to your house, and free access to everything in your home, which could be a security concern. Thefts can occur that way, especially if she lends the keys or copies them for someone else. Or, you have to arrange to be home whenever she's scheduled to be there. That ties you down to a schedule, which you may or may not like. And, if one of her kids gets sick, she may not show up, and she may not call, but you still have to be there as if she were going to come. Your time will therefore no longer be your own, to a certain extent.

The same is true for gardeners who have to go through your house to get to the back or side yard. And if it turns out to be a housekeeper or gardener you're not fond of, you don't have the authority to make a change. You can, of course, complain to your landlord, but that could just make for more discomfort. So, do think about these issues before signing a lease.

If you want to hire your own domestic help, you will have more flexibility. First, only hire one that comes well recommended from someone you trust. Since you're a newcomer, that will probably be your rental agent, someone at the Lake Chapala Society, or a friend who has lived here longer.

Never hire anyone who simply knocks on your door and seems to be desperate, hoping you'll feel sorry for them. Local people who are good and honest don't resort to that since they have extended families that have their own connections.

And don't hire people from ads or postings. Only trust word of mouth recommendations from people you trust. Remember that anyone you hire will learn a great deal about you, including your relative wealth, how to get access to your home, the value of your belongings, and your schedule.

These same guidelines apply to general handy men, too. Your landlord or agency will know whom to trust. Plus, there are recommendations on the local online web boards (see Appendix).

When hiring a new person, make a copy of their official Mexican identification, which is their IFE voting credential. They should all have one. Also make a copy of the person's recent utility bill, verifying where they live.

Pets

The Lake Chapala area has everything you need for your pets. There are lovely parks to walk your dog in, like Cristiania Park in Chapala, and the various *malecónes* along the coast. The only problems you'll find are the stray dogs that hang out in these areas. They won't necessarily cause any problems, because they're quite well socialized to other dogs and people. It's just that they tend to follow other dogs that they like. So, it can be a nuisance. At worst, you may have to cut your walk short, and find another spot.

> *"Remember that anyone you hire will learn a great deal about you, including your relative wealth, how to get access to your home, the value of your belongings, and your schedule."*

There are various animal shelters and outreach programs in the area that take homeless, abused, and injured animals (mostly dogs) off the streets, and try to prepare them for adoption. They're wonderful organizations – usually non-profits – worthy of charitable contributions, if you're so inclined. Despite their best efforts, you will still see some very scruffy dogs on the streets. Some have homes, and some simply live on the streets. In some areas, butchers (*carnicerías*) provide them with daily scraps, and the dogs line up like school-children there for their handouts.

Regarding pet health care, there are plenty of very competent English-speaking veterinarians all along the *carretera*. The local web boards can provide up-to-date recommendations for you. You will also find very good pet foods, including north of the border brands at the *supermercados,* and at pet stores. You'll even find high-end brands like Science Diet, IAMS, and specialty diets in some pet stores, like the Animal Shelter A.C. Pet Store in Riberas Del Pilar at 212 Hidalgo (the *carretera*) between Calle San Lucas and Calle San Mateo. That store also carries good flea and tick repellents like Front-line Plus. My own dogs and cats were flea magnets north of the border, a situation which was controlled very well by Front-Line Plus. None of them have needed the medication here, for some reason. I may simply be in an area where there are few fleas and ticks, or there may simply be fewer of them in general.

As for grooming, there are excellent pet services here. The one I recommend is called Furry Friends, run by two sisters, right along the *carretera* in the colonia of Mirasol in Ajijic. The address is Bugambilias #11. The whole works for a dog costs about $15 USD. I've been very pleased with the results, and my dogs love them.

Cooking

One of the reasons the Lake Chapala area has such a temperate climate (as opposed to the Mexican coasts, which can be hot and humid) is that it is situated high in the mountains – 5,000 feet above sea level – about the same as Denver. But for that reason, you may need to adjust the way you cook and bake. High-altitude cooking is the opposite of pressure cooking. The boiling point of water is lower because there is less air pressure, so foods that are boiled will need longer cooking times since they're using a lower temperature. Here is a website from the US government: http://tinyurl.com/d67yr8b. Similarly for baking, liquids evaporate faster since it takes less heat for water to start boiling. In addition, leavening agents (like yeast) expand faster. Here's an informative website for high-altitude baking: www.highaltitudebaking.com.

Mail Services

The Mexican government, like every other country's government, provides postal services. From my own experiences and from the other expats I've talked to, they do a pretty good job. Postal carriers, usually on foot or on motorcycles, will put your envelopes and flyers (very few of these, thank goodness) in your mailbox, or slide them under your door – Monday through Saturday. For packages, they will give you a slip of paper indicating that a box is waiting for you at the post office, and it will have the address of the post office on it.

So, why would you need mail services aside from that? The primary reason is that, because of customs at the border, it takes about 2 weeks for letters and packages from north of the border to arrive from the time it was sent. So, if you buy something from eBay, for instance (making sure they'll ship to Mexico), you'll have to wait for them to process the order and ship it, and then you'll have to wait 2 weeks for it to be delivered. That could easily mean a wait of 3 weeks. The reverse is true, too. It takes about 2 weeks for items to reach the US and Canada.

For outgoing mail, one of the ways to speed up the process is to drop your mail off (envelopes only) at the Lake Chapala Society office – but only if you're a member. Other members who are going across the border will take the envelopes with them, and deposit them in a mailbox in the US. That cuts the delivery time down to a few days rather than a few weeks, and you only need a US stamp, so you don't need to pay international rates.

If the company you're buying something from north of the border does not ship to Mexico, then you'll want to have a north of the border address. You can, of course, use the address of a friend or family member, who then has to take the time to re-wrap the package, re-address the package, and then go to a post office to ship it to your address here. You probably would not want to ask them to do that for you very often. And, they may not be as speedy as you'd like in getting that done.

So, instead, a mail service here can provide that function for you. You'll be given a post office box in Texas to which your mail, including packages, can be delivered. The mail services' agents there in Texas take your mail though customs, and cause it to be delivered to your mail service outlet here, from which you can pick it up. If it's regular first class mail, it takes about the same time as it would if it were sent directly to you. The advantage is that the sender only has to ship it to Texas, and only has to pay for it going that far. That means you can still get your magazines and newspaper subscriptions, if you want, since they don't normally deliver across borders. You end up paying for the rest of the trip, though, and for any customs duties, and for the service when you pick up the items.

Other reasons to use mail services is that they can provide you with a post office box, they can help with shipping materials, and they use public and private carriers, like USPS, UPS, DHL, and FedEx.

The three most popular mail services at Lakeside are:

- Mailboxes, Etc. – Carretera #144, San Antonio. The cross street is Calle Glez. Gallo.
- Sol y Luna – inside the Bugambilias Plaza at the corner of Revolución and the *carretera* in Ajijic.
- HandyMail – one block west of Mailboxes, Etc. inside a hardware store between Calle Glez. Gallo and Calle Independencía.

You'll want to compare the services, hours, and rates by visiting them and getting their rate sheets. And, you'll want to review the experiences expats have had with them by visiting the local web boards (see Appendix).

Garbage Pickup

Each town has its own garbage pickup services, and they're free – being paid for, presumably, by property taxes. The big garbage trucks roll around the streets at least several times per week at different times of the day. Garbage is picked up every other day in some towns, and every day in others. Everything except very large items seems to be picked up, including yard waste. Most people just put out their plastic bags by the curb. But, in areas where there are street dogs, some people use plastic trash cans, or they hang the bags from tree limbs. You'll want to just follow what your neighbors do in this regard.

You'll also want to consider separating recyclables from regular garbage. Some of the locals will pick them up in order to get the deposits from the recycling centers. If you don't separate them, some locals will actually go through your trash themselves, and pick out the cans and bottles.

Beauty Salons and Barbers

For women, there are lots of beauty salons which offer all the hair, nail, and spa services you're used to north of the border. You'll find that the quality of the services is very good, and that every shop has at least one person who speaks English. The prices are lower than comparable services north of the border. You'll see some salons along the *carretera*, but there are many interspersed within the towns, as well.

Men can also use these salons, of course, but there are also many traditional barbershops.

Tipping is customary for all the services – between 10 and 15%. To find good recommendations for these services, check the web boards (see Appendix).

Chapter 9

Utilities

Your home utilities at Lakeside are fairly straightforward, once you know how they operate.

Gas

The simplest of the household utilities is gas for cooking and water heating. Because there is no Lakeside-wide underground gas pipe system, every house has its own gas tank – usually on the roof. This is replenished, when requested, by independent services that come to your house and fill up the tank. The gas trucks are easy to find since they make regular rounds in the neighborhoods, usually with music playing. You may want to ask your landlord or previous house owner who provided the services in the past, and whether they recommend continuing with that company. When you first move in, you'll want to have someone check the gas level in the tank to make sure you're not about to run out.

> *"When you first move in, you'll want to have someone check the gas level in the tank to make sure you're not about to run out."*

Compared with electricity at Lakeside, gas is very inexpensive. If you have a choice of gas or electric appliances, like clothes dryers or stoves or even portable heaters, choose the gas ones.

Water

Unless you have a water well, your household water is piped in from your town. But it isn't pumped in 24 hours per day – due to cost constraints. It's usually pumped in starting in the early morning until mid-afternoon. It goes into a cistern (*aljibe*) on your property, where it stays until the roof-top water tank (*tinaco*) gets low, at which time a pump starts pumping water from the cistern to the water tank to replenish it. For that reason, you'll want to do your laundry and lawn watering early in the day rather than later. The water pressure in your house is (usually) based on gravity from the water falling from the roof-top tank, so you'll find that the water pressure from your taps, shower, and washing machine is less than what you're used to north of the border.

> *"Your tap water is not considered potable (drinkable) no matter how clean the water was when it was piped in from the town."*

Since this way of receiving and storing water is not a closed system, your tap water is not considered potable (drinkable) no matter how clean the water was when it was piped in from the town. Both the cistern and the water tank need to be cleaned every six months to a year, and filters replaced. You can also add chlorine tablets to the cistern, if you'd like.

If you rent your house, this maintenance is usually scheduled and paid for by your landlord. The water itself is also usually paid for by the landlord so you won't be tempted to skimp on watering the garden. Water is actually fairly inexpensive at Lakeside. If you own your home, check with the previous owner regarding system maintenance, and water billing from the town. You can also research various places that can install water purification systems and/or water pressure systems in your house. The local web boards (see the Appendix) have very good information on these.

Electricity

Electricity is considered fairly expensive at Lakeside (based on the general cost of living here), and most people (expats and locals) minimize its use whenever possible. For instance, the new compact fluorescent (CFL) spiral light bulbs are used much more frequently here than north of the border. The electricity is turned on 24 hours per day, so there does not seem to be a shortage of it. Outages do occur, but only during severe storms or utility pole accidents, and then usually not for long.

> *"Electric volts and plugs are exactly the same as north of the border, with both 2-plug and 3-plug wall plates, so adapters are not needed."*

Electric volts and plugs are exactly the same as north of the border, with both 2-plug and 3-plug wall plates, so adapters are not needed. Most houses have a grounding wire from the roof to a metal pole in the soil to protect against lightning. It's always a good idea to use surge protectors for your technical devices, of course, but I haven't found it necessary to have brown-out protectors or a UPS system. But these might be good insurance if you're running a technology company out of your home.

The CFE (*Comisión Federal de Electicidad*) is a government-owned utility, and it sends an electric bill every two months to either you or your landlord. The amount charged is based on how much you use according to your house's electric meter readings, just like north of the border. There are three rate levels for home use (*doméstico*). You will be charged .743 pesos for each of the first 150 kilowatt hours used in the two month period. You will be charged .903 pesos for each of the next 128 kilowatt hours, and you will be charged 2.619 pesos for each of the next 278 kilowatt hours. But, if you exceed an accumulated 3,000 kilowatt hours any time between January and December, your classification will change from a *doméstico* to a DAC (De Alto Consumo), and you will have to pay much more. That's because the government subsidizes all *domésticos* – by about 75%. As an example, my own electric bill for April to June of 2012 shows I consumed 278 kilowatt hours, and that the cost of production for that was 1,100 pesos (about $85 USD). The government paid the first 873 pesos (about $67 USD), so my final bill came to 264 pesos (about $20 USD) – for two months. That's very inexpensive by my standards, but for some locals, that's plenty.

Homes that have water purification systems, swimming, pools, and water pressure pumps, as well as air conditioning in summer and portable electric heaters in the winter are the ones who tend to reach the DAC level, and thereby lose their subsidy. What some people do to avoid that is to change the account name to their spouse half-way through the year. That resets the counter back to zero. If the DAC level has been reached, though, it will stay that way until 3 two-month bills (6 months' worth) show a lower use consistent with the *doméstico* level. You will then be a *doméstico* again, and the subsidy will start again.

Solar Energy

The green movement is in full swing at Lakeside, so solar energy is starting to be used here now. There are several companies in the area. You'll want to check the local web boards and magazines (see the Appendix) for their names and reviews. Solar energy may make financial sense only if you own your home, and if you plan to stay for a long time, in order to recoup the initial investment.

As stated earlier, Mexico does have a consumer protection agency called PROFECO, if you want to file a complaint against a merchant. The website for more information is: www.profeco.gob.mx/english.htm.

Chapter 10

Technology

Advanced technologies for land phones, cell phones, TV, internet, personal computers, smart phones, and tablets are relatively new at Lakeside. As you may imagine, this is where your life can get very complicated. Unlike most of the offerings north of the border, some of the technology choices here don't actually work very well – or as you expected. As a newcomer, you can spend months fuming and switching services until you get just the right mix of what you want. To minimize that as much as possible, here are some tips.

Land Phone

If your home came with a land phone (i.e., wired from the street), you probably have TelMex service. That's the standard Mexican fixed-line carrier. It's a privately owned company, but it's fairly close to being a monopoly. If you decide to remove your TelMex service, they will not only disconnect you electronically at the switching station, they'll come and physically remove the cabling, as well. Most people don't want that, for fear that switching back to TelMex might take a long time because of the cabling. Starting service for a brand new home does take awhile, too, for that reason. The good news is that the TelMex service is pretty good. You can have the service options you're used to north of the border, as well, like call forwarding, call waiting, and voicemail. I haven't experienced or heard of any dial tone or dropped call complaints. You can get different plans, of course, for a variety of prices, and they're fairly inexpensive.

What can get expensive, though, is international calling. If you call the US or other countries often, you may want to consider signing up with Skype (it's computer based, and free). Some people use Vonage, although, compared to other options, it's fairly expensive. Plus there have been connection problems and line quality problems reported with Vonage. Magic Jack (computer required), or Magic Jack Plus (no computer required), NetTalk, and Packet8 are other popular options here. As a newcomer, if you just want a no-headaches home phone for awhile until the rest of your technology is stabilized, stick with TelMex. After you've settled, you may want to research other technology options for your international calls. If all else fails, or in a pinch, HandyMail offers free international calls from their phone. They're located on the *carretera* inside a hardware store between Calle Glez. Gallo and Calle Independencía in San Antonio.

Internet

TelMex also has internet services – both dial-up and DSL (called Infinitum). If you're not too fussy about internet speed, these would be good choices. There have been many complaints, however, that the promised TelMex DSL speeds (you can sign up for different speeds) never quite get there. Again, this may not be a problem for you – and, you may be able to take advantage of TelMex's land-phone and internet bundled plans.

There's another popular wireless internet service provider in the area called Lagunanet that you'll want to inquire about. The website is laguna.com.mx.

If internet speed is important to you, you'll want to consider the offerings of Telecable. They're the only cable company in the area, but they have an inconsistent record. Sometimes the service drops, and you just have to wait until it comes back online. Usually, that only takes a few minutes, but sometimes it takes hours and even days – especially when Telecable is expanding their territory, which they're currently in the process of doing. When it works, it's great. But because it's not always available, some people also subscribe to TelMex's Infinitum as a backup system. That way, they can also send a support email to Telecable to alert them about the outage. Whenever Telecable comes back from an outage, by the way, I find that I always have to unplug and re-plug my modem and router.

> *"When you get internet service in Mexico, you may no longer be able to view internet content that is copyrighted only for the US market."*

When you get internet service in Mexico, you may no longer be able to view internet content that is copyrighted only for the US market. And, a good deal of the content will be automatically translated into Spanish for you. That's because you now have a Mexican IP address for your computer, which the internet sites read in order to determine where you are, what they can show you, and in what language. For example, if you go to Netflix, you'll only see the DVDs authorized to be shown in Mexico. That is, for the streaming versions only. Netflix doesn't mail DVDs in Mexico. Some sites may not be available at all, like Hulu and Hulu Plus, Vudu, and Pandora Radio.

There are several ways to make websites think you're in the US, though. One way is to buy a router with an American IP from a place like Momentum Technologies (www.huluenmexico.com). It costs less than $20. Another way is to subscribe to a proxy service that has an American IP. The one I use is Easy Hide IP (www.easy-hide-ip.com). It costs $29, which is well worth it for me. You can do a free trial of it, too, so you can see the results. An added advantage to using a proxy service is that it makes you anonymous on the internet. But, sometimes I have to switch it back to my Mexican IP address (it's very easy to do) because some of the sites I like actually require that I not be in the US. One of these is USTVNow (see the section on TV).

iTunes is also tricky. It actually doesn't use your IP address to determine your location. It uses your billing credit card's address. Mine happens to be Mexican. So, it assumes I'm in Mexico, and will only show me titles authorized to be distributed in Mexico (there are a lot fewer of them). And, all the iTunes pages are in Spanish, too. I could change the credit card to my US card, but then I can't purchase anything because I discontinued funding that card (it was really a debit card). So, this is another reason to keep at least one US credit card alive.

Radio

There is very little of interest that's loud enough to hear on traditional radio here at Lakeside. That includes both FM and AM. The problem is not that there are no stations playing, it's that the reception is poor due to the surrounding mountains.

In fact, when I need to set my alarm (which isn't often here in Mexico), I have to set it on buzzer, since I can't be sure of what station will be audible in the morning. Your car radio will be almost useless in this area, except for the speakers for playing your favorite CDs. However, you may be able to stream your favorite radio stations on the internet, and then play them on your portable devices, like your smart phone or your tablet. For instance, iTunes streams NPR (National Public Radio) stations live from all over the US.

TV

I don't recommend buying a phone-internet-TV bundle with Telecable. They don't currently offer a phone voicemail service (they don't tell you that up front), which I found unacceptable for my needs – after they had put up new phone wiring. And the only reason you would want their TV service is to receive a few local US TV channels (which you can get in other ways – see below). They receive the local US channels from the US Dish satellite network, and the visual quality is poor, and often unavailable. So, I would only recommend the internet service from Telecable at this time.

> *"Be aware, though, that US media companies have different programming for Mexico."*

There are other satellite network TV offerings here that are pretty reliable – including HD (High Definition). Shaw Network is very well liked, but you have to buy a receiver and a large satellite dish. It's a Canadian company, but equipment can be purchased in Guadalajara at CP Electronics. For more information, their website is here: www.cp-electronics.com/eng/index.php. Check the local web boards for more information about this option, and to inquire about used equipment and service plans.

SKY satellite network is also good. They will come and install the dish free of charge – IF you sign an 18 month contract. They have various package deals with various channel groupings, many of which have US channels and premium channels. There's a good mixture of Mexican and US channels available. Be aware though, that US media companies have different programming for Mexico. So, you're not necessarily going to get first-run programming on HBO, for instance. SKY just airs whatever HBO chooses to send them, which may or may not be what people in the US are seeing. Sometimes the CNN channel airs CNN US, and sometimes it airs CNN International. And the Fox station plays a lot of The Simpsons reruns. There is no documented schedule, either. You can see a day's schedule by clicking the Guide button on the remote, but it's often incorrect. So, basically, you get what you get.

Regarding payments: you can have SKY automatically charge your monthly fee to your credit card, but they won't accept debit cards, except over the phone. With all these caveats, I still find SKY a good choice for me. Their website is www2.sky.com.mx/mexico, and their English-speaking phone number for customers is 800-475-9759. They even have a Tivo option for recording programs.

The DirecTV Mexico satellite network is available here, but it has mostly Spanish channels. The US DirecTV offerings used to be available only in the US, but since they've switched satellites, it's now possible to get reception Lakeside, although you'll need to get assistance with the equipment requirements. Assistance can be found on the web boards (see the Appendix), where at least a few satellite tech people tune in.

The Dish Mexico (www.dishmexico.com) satellite network is also available here. You'll want to compare its offerings with the others. I suspect it's similar to SKY, but I haven't tried it because I was so disappointed with the quality of the local US channels that Telecable offered via Dish. Again, you'll want to find out whether the channels (like Fox, HBO, and CNN) air the same streams that are shown in the US, or whether the streams consist mostly of reruns. You'll also want to ask whether programming schedules are available. And, you'll want to find out which channels are in Spanish, which are in English, which are in Spanish with English subtitles, and which are in English with Spanish subtitles. You'll probably find, as I unexpectedly did, that you'll come to appreciate programming in English with Spanish subtitles to help you learn Spanish.

There are many live-streaming US (and maybe Canadian) TV channels available on the internet – both nationally broadcast channels, as well as cable. The one I use is USTVNow (www.ustvnow.com). You can get the basic package for free, which includes ABC, CBS, CW, FOX, NBC, and PBS. You have to have a non-US IP address in order for it to work. There are also fee-based packages that include cable stations and HD – and even a recording function for the channels. You have to have a fairly fast (I recommend at least 8MB) internet service, though, for this to be useful. Otherwise, the video will spend more time getting hung up than playing. I've also found a free live stream of MSNBC at www.themonspot.com/msnbc-alt.html. You will see an advertisement in front of the video screen for a few seconds, but then you can close it.

Cell Phones

When you first move to Lake Chapala, you can use your existing north of the border cell phone, using its roaming feature for both voice and text messaging. But you'll want to turn that feature off except when you're actually using it because it's expensive. It not just expensive when you're using it, it's expensive when you're not using it (if you have the phone in stand-by mode) because cell phones communicate a great deal with their providers – updating location information and applications, and monitoring minutes left.

Because of the expense of continually using a north-of-the-border cell phone, you'll want to research your best reasonable option for getting a Mexican one – either as a replacement, or as an additional one. The four main cell phone carriers in this area are:

- TelCel
- Unefon
- Movistar
- IUSACELL

Cell phone calls all go through Guadalajara, which is why they have different city codes than land phones here (see the Index for Telephone Dialing).

Some people swear by each of the above carriers, so which one to choose is really a matter of personal preference, including who has the best service plan for voice and data at the time, who gets the best reception in which areas, who has an area-wide 3G network, and who is using GSM. Because these factors change over time, my advice is to look on the local web boards (see the Appendix) for the most up-to-date information.

As for myself, I came to this area with an iPhone locked into Verizon service. I was told that most people use TelCel, but when I went to a TelCel office (they're everywhere, but they don't often have English speakers), they said they couldn't convert my phone because it would require a new SIM card, and mine had no SIM slot. They said Unefon didn't require a SIM card, though. The Unefon counter I then went to is inside Walmart. They said they could convert the phone, but that it would take several weeks. I didn't want to be without it for that long, so I decided to buy an inexpensive phone with Unefon service (it cost a little less per call, as I remember). But, the phone was unable to get a Unefon signal inside of Walmart, so I went back to TelCel, and finally bought a cheap cell phone with TelCel pay-as-you-go service. I still carry both phones, and cancelled the US Verizon service. I can add more minutes to my TelCel phone by paying money through many local merchants, like Walmart. All I need to do is hand them my cell phone number and some money, and the number of minutes available increases.

Be aware that with TelCel, you have to add money to the account at least every two months, otherwise your service is disconnected until you add more money. You never actually lose your minutes, you just can't use them unless you keep adding something (a minimum of 100 pesos, I think) every two months. You can see how many minutes you have left by pressing 133#, but it'll cost you $.88 USD to do it. A free way to see how many minutes you have left is to go here: www.mitelcel.com/mitelcel/login/auth.

By the way, if you receive a call on your Mexican cell phone, you'll be charged. Both the sender and the receiver pay.

When you get a TelCel phone, you're automatically signed up to be sent lots of text messages in Spanish, which they don't tell you about up front. Some of the messages are about the news, but most are advertisements. Even though they don't cost you any airtime, you'll want to get rid of most of these because they're a nuisance. When you get one of those, reply to it with the word BAJA in capital letters. That's supposed to unsubscribe you. There's one kind, though, that can't be eliminated, and that's from TelCel, offering you a 2-for-1 offer on your purchase of more minutes. If you have trouble eliminating the other ones, go to the TelCel office in the block west of the Bugambilias Plaza, on the corner of the *carretera* and Juan Alvarez street. It's in a little mini-mall next to the Crown Casino (yes, we have those, too, here). There is at least one person in that TelCel office who speaks English, which isn't the case in many of their other offices. She can eliminate those messages for you.

The decision around cell phones can make you crazy in a hurry, if you let it, because the options and the specials and the plans and the phones change frequently. Dare to opt for "good enough".

Smart Phones and Tablets

As with most electronics, you'll pay a lower price in the US because of the customs fees merchants have to pay to get them imported to Mexico. Plus, there's a 16% sales tax in Mexico (in some areas near the border, it's less). So, it's generally wiser to bring your electronics with you when you move to this area – unless you're moving from somewhere other than north of the border.

Smart phones and tablets are really small computers, so everything noted in the section above regarding the internet applies to these devices, too. That is, the internet will know you're in Mexico unless you use a service or router that hides your true location by masking your IP address. And, the speed of the internet and emailing will depend on the speed of the internet service you sign up for through Telecable or TelMex, or some other ISP provider.

Chapter 11

Banking

As with the technology sector, the banking industry Lakeside is not quite what you are used to north of the border. They seem to have the technology, but it isn't as stable, and they are not as focused on the customer experience as they are north of the border. At least that has been my experience to date.

As mentioned earlier, you'll want to keep at least one north-of-the-border credit card as a backup, at least for awhile, until you're confident about your new Mexican banking arrangements – or permanently. There's no downside to using your north of the border credit card, except that you'll have to keep remembering the north of the border address and phone number that you used to open up that credit card account with every time you use it as a "billing address" online. By the way, the only US credit card I'm aware of that does not charge an international usage fee is CapitalOne. You may want to research that as one of your options.

If you have a PayPal account, you may want to keep that open, too, for online purchases made north of the border, too. The reason for that is that the debit card you will get from a Lakeside bank may or may not work online.

For instance, the bank account I got from Banamex here is considered a debit *checking* account (although I don't get any checks). It has a MasterCard logo on it, and I can use it anywhere, even online in the US. On the other hand, the account I got from Bancomer here is considered a debit *savings* account (although it does not earn interest), and it has a Visa logo on it, but it cannot be used online for purchases.

Why would I get both a Banamex account and a Bancomer account? I want to keep my Banamex account because I have it linked to my Banamex USA Money Market account (called an Amistad account) in San Diego, where my social security benefits get deposited automatically. The transfer of funds from the San Diego account to the Lakeside account is free, and takes 5 minutes. And, if the value of the peso or the dollar changes significantly, I can move money back and forth very easily. But, I have had so many problems with Banamex here that I have all but given up on them.

Suffice it to say that one of the major problems at Banamex is that they do not want to pay their staff the extra expense to hire English speakers. I learned this directly from my account representative, who is only one of two English speakers on the floor. When they are ill or out to lunch or on vacation or their accounts get locked up, nothing gets done for expats who aren't fluent in Spanish. I also learned from my representative that Banamex will only issue true credit cards to expats with FM-2 (not FM-3) visas. Another problem at Banamex is that their systems are sometimes unavailable – even within the bank.

Hence, my new Bancomer account. My short experience with Bancomer has been more productive. My debit card account with them, called an *El Libretón* account, is the only one Walmart will allow to provide cash back at cash registers. I can take out up to 2,000 pesos (about $175 USD) in cash as I'm paying for my purchases there. And, I found out from my account representative at Bancomer that they do issue true credit cards to expats with an FM-3 visa after about 6 months (on request). They look at your Mexican credit rating and your average balance, and give you a commensurate credit limit to start with. That's a good way to start building credit in Mexico. There are three downsides to this account, however.

1. There's a minimum monthly average balance requirement of 1,000 pesos, or they assess a monthly service charge of 150 pesos.
2. They don't have a north of the border bank from which you can do direct money transfers without a fee. They do have a partnership with Wells Fargo Bank, but the ability to conduct direct transfers is not one of the functions.
3. The debit card cannot be used for online transactions.

You will need to assess your own banking needs, of course, in order to determine your best set of banking options. Not everyone has had the experiences I described above. And, there are other major banks here, including HSBC (which has been in the news recently regarding money laundering),

Santander, and ScotiaBank. Bank of America has some arrangements with both Santander and ScotiaBank that may be worth investigating. There are also investment companies locally. You'll want to search the local web boards for more information on these, and for others' experiences.

> *"There is no reason why you can't use only your own north of the border bank's services and credit/debit cards here, thereby avoiding any need to deal with a Mexican bank."*

Again, there is no reason why you can't use only your own north of the border bank's services and credit/debit cards here, thereby avoiding any need to deal with a Mexican bank. You can withdraw money from an ATM here at quite a good exchange rate, and the ATM fees are about the same as they are north of the border – about $2.50 USD. The downsides are:

1. You won't have an opportunity to build a Mexican credit history. But, you wouldn't want to take out a loan from a Mexican bank because their rates aren't very good. So, having a Mexican credit history may not be of much importance to you.
2. You can only withdraw up to a certain daily limit from an ATM. That's usually between $500 and $700 USD.

3. You can do a wire transfer from your north of the border bank to places at Lakeside (like banks or at Walmart), but you'll be charged a transfer fee (around $15 USD).

Speaking of ATMs, you'll want to use the ATM at your bank's location whenever possible since it has the least possibility of being tampered with. Also, do withdraw enough cash from your ATM on Fridays to cover you through the weekend, since some of the ATMs run out of cash before Monday morning.

By the way, you may not use a cell phone in a bank. This includes both placing a call and answering a call. If your cell phone rings in a bank, just let it ring. You may not answer it. This rule is to prevent someone inside a bank from tipping off someone outside the bank when a patron withdraws a large amount of money.

Mexican bank accounts are secured by a government organization similar to USA's FDIC (Federal Deposit Insurance Corporation). It's called IPAB, and the current savings protection is up to 1.9 million pesos per account. The website is here: www.ipab.org.mx

There's also a government agency called CONDUSEF, through which you can file a complaint against a Mexican financial institution. Its website is: www.condusef.gob.mx. This agency is very powerful, and can convince a bank that is reluctant to settle a claim that it's in its best financial interest to do so.

Chapter 12

Government Services

You will most likely come into contact with many government services at Lakeside. Most of them are well run, and are staffed with at least one English-speaker. With a little preparation on your part, these services will be a great benefit to you.

Visas

The following descriptions of the most common expat visas are accurate as of the publication date of this book. However, new visa laws are expected to be implemented within the next six months. Updates will be made in future editions of this book. In the mean time, I plan to post updates to this website as soon as the information is available: www.MovingToMexicosLakeChapala.com.

> *"New visa laws are expected to be implemented within the next six months."*

Here's an explanation of the most common visas.

- FMM – this is really not a visa. It's a tourist card. It's the one you get when you cross the border into Mexico. It is a small green and peach-colored piece of paper called a *Forma Migratoria Multiple*. You can Google that to see images of what it looks like. You can get along with just this for up to 180 days at a time. Then you'll need to cross to the US again (surrendering your FMM tourist card and vehicle permit), and get another set for another 180 days when you make a U-turn back into Mexico. You can do this forever, if you want, and there's no need to inform the immigration department where you're located within Mexico any time within the 180 days. But, it's inconvenient to have to re-cross the border if you plan to stay.

- FM-3 – this is called a *"No Inmigrante"* visa, and needs to be renewed every year for a maximum of 5 years, after which time you can start another 5 year period, if you still qualify. It may or may not include a working permit depending on the type applied for, but one is possible with proper application to the Mexican government
- FM-2 – this is called an *"Inmigrante"*, and is similar to a "Green Card" in the US. Like the FM-3 visa, it may or may not include a working permit, depending on the type applied for, but one is possible with proper application to the Mexican government. Under current law, FM-2 holders are restricted in their time spent outside Mexico, only being allowed to be gone 18 months in a 5 year period. Also, only the *"rentista"* (retiree) type may legally have a foreign-plated car. The FM-2 is the type of visa where after 5 years you may apply for citizenship, or after only 2 years if you're married to a Mexican, or born in a Latin American country.

To avoid having to re-cross the border every 180 days, to be able to open a Mexican checking or savings account in most Mexican banks, and to qualify for Mexican discount cards like the INAPAM and the DIF cards, and IMSS and Seguro Popular insurance policies, most expats choose to apply for an FM-3 visa soon after they arrive.

You could also get an FM-3 visa before arriving at the border by downloading the online application, and going to a Mexican embassy or consulate in your home country. But, you'll have to go through a process when you get here to update your address, among other things, so there's really no advantage to doing it before you get here. You would be spending more time, and possible double fees by doing it advance.

You must earn a certain amount of money outside of Mexico, such as from the US Social Security Administration, pension, retirement, or a job in the US. For 2012, the minimum income is approximately 15,582.50 pesos (approximately $1,100 USD) per month. The reason it's approximate is that it depends on the currency exchange rate, plus each immigration office is allowed to adapt the figure to local conditions.

Most *abogados* can either just prepare the paperwork for you, so you can submit it to immigration yourself, or they can prepare the paperwork plus accompany you through the whole process. You will want to do the latter if you have complicating factors like dependents – especially if you're renewing your visa close to the time when it will expire.

For your yearly FM-3 renewals, be sure to start the process about a month in advance so your visa doesn't expire. Not only will you be in the country illegally if it does, you will lose your vehicle deposit. Your vehicle deposit will go straight to the Mexican government as soon as your tourist card or visa expires. This is definitely one case of Mexican efficiency.

> *"For your yearly FM-3 renewals, be sure to start the process about a month in advance so your visa doesn't expire."*

It's best not to travel out of the country during the last 30 days before your visa expires, just to be sure you don't get locked out of the country because of any processing delays. The process itself (whether initial or renewal) only takes two weeks or so if there are no complicating factors. You can keep renewing your FM-3 visa forever, if you want, as long as you still qualify.

Instead of getting an FM-3 visa right away, you can choose to get an FM-2 visa, instead. Or, you can do that later. You might want to do that if you know you're going to stay in Mexico permanently. You still have to renew it every year, but you can apply for Mexican citizenship (without losing your original citizenship) after 5 years on the FM-2 visa.

But, with an FM-2 visa,

- you cannot have a foreign-plated car, unless you have *"rentista"*-type FM-2. There are different classes of FM-2s.
- you must have a minimum foreign monthly income of around 24,932 pesos ($1,883 USD).
- if you stay outside of Mexico for longer than 18 months in a five-year period, except under exceptional circumstances, you will lose your right to be a citizen or *inmigrado* at the end of the 5-year period.

The immigration office in Chapala is located on the *carretera* at 271 Hidalgo. The building won't say "Immigration" on it. It will have signs saying SEGOB INM, and the INM part is stylized in a logo that's difficult to read. It's open from about 9am to 1pm Mondays through Fridays. Because it's a federal facility, don't be alarmed to find two armed guards outside. The best way to locate the building is to drive east on the *carretera* into Chapala. Right outside the SEGOB INM building there are brightly colored triangular flags strung high overhead across the street - from one side of the street to the other – just like you see sometimes for used car dealerships. You can certainly visit them to ask any questions you might have.

INAPAM and DIF Senior Discount Cards

One of the benefits of obtaining an FM-3 or FM-2 visa is that you can get two free discount cards - if you're over 60. The INAPAM organization is like the federal government's version of the US's AARP, and the card is just one of the benefits the organization offers. You can get 10% – 15% off participating movie theaters, and 50% off buses, including both the local buses Lakeside and bus tours. It's also good at some airlines, at Guadalajara's zoo, at the Walmart pharmacy, and at Farmácia Guadalajara. There are three of these pharmacies on the *carretera* – one in Chapala near the SEGOB INM building (see previous section on Visas), one in Ajijic at the corner of Guerra street, and one in Jocotepec.

The DIF card is similar to the INAPAM card, except that it's run by the state's social services department, rather than the federal government. Some places take one or the other, or both. It never hurts to ask your merchants if they honor them. You will be surprised how many of them do.

If you're planning to go on a bus trip, be aware that there are only a certain number of DIF/INAPAM seats available per trip. So, you'll want to purchase your tickets in advance to ensure you get one of the discounted seats.

Both cards are permanent; they never need to be renewed.

Here is where to get both cards in Chapala.

DIF/INAPAM Office
Degollado #327, Chapala
Phone Number: 376-765-3349
Hours: Mondays and Tuesdays from 9am to 2pm

Directions : Going toward Chapala on the *carretera*, turn left at the Madero stoplight. Turn right two blocks north of the Plaza (Degollado). Continue on Degollado (you will cross Juarez, Zaragoza, and 5 de Mayo). The building is on your left in the middle of the following block next to the Chapala Post Office.

You need to bring:

1. the original and 2 copies of your FM-3 or FM-2 card. Make sure each copy has an image of the front and the back of the card on the same page.
2. your passport and 2 copies of the photo and signature page of it.
3. 4 *infantile*-size (small) color photos of yourself. You must be facing forward. You can get these at Walmart or Farmácia Guadalajara for about 50 pesos.
4. a recent proof of residence document. This can be an electric bill, or a TelMex or TV service bill, like Telecable. If you don't have one of these in your own name, they'll take one in your landlord's name.
5. You must know your blood type. A simple blood test taken at any laboratory for less than $10 USD can inform you of this, if you don't know it. They don't require proof.

Driver's License

You must have an unexpired driver's license if you drive a car in Mexico. The license can be from a foreign country, though. Check with your former country to find out if yours can be renewed by mail. If not, it's time to get a Mexican driver's license – as long as you have an FM-2 or an FM-3 visa. If you don't, you'll have to go back to your home country to have your license renewed. At Lakeside, the place to get your Mexican license is *Gobierno del Edo De Jalisco Sria. De Vialidad y Transporte*. It's located at 405 Flavio Romero de Velasco in central Chapala. That's on the northeast corner where it meets Guerrero. The hours are 9am to 2pm weekdays. It's best to show up early to make sure you can get it all done in one day. The requirements to get a Mexican driver's license are:

- You must be 18 years of age or older.
- You must bring your passport and one black & white copy of the face page.
- You must have your FM-3 or FM-2 visa and one black & white copy.
- You must know your blood type.
- You must have proof of residence and one black & white copy. This can be a utility bill, telephone bill, water bill, or a Mexican bank statement, none of which can be more than 90 days old.
- You must pass a vision test.
- You must pass a road test.
- You must pass a written test. There will be an English translator there, if you need one.

Moving to Mexico's Lake Chapala

- You must pay a 435 pesos fee (239 pesos for a motorcycle license) if you pass the tests.

Here are the official 103 driving regulation questions and answers in Spanish, **only 20 of which** will be on the written test.

http://tinyurl.com/7wehswe

And here is the English translation of the 103 questions.

http://tinyurl.com/8db4cg9

You can choose to get a regular driver's license or a *"chofer"* (chauffer) license. Choose the *"chofer"* license because you won't be allowed to drive a pick-up truck without it. The test questions are the same, so you might as well get the *"chofer"*.

> *"You must have your original driver's license with you whenever you drive."*

When you take the test, it'll be in Spanish, so it's best if you can read the questions in both languages. There will be an English interpreter available for you, though, when you take your test, if you need one.

Just one note: when you take your driving test, make sure you turn on your blinking hazard lights whenever you back up.

Also, you must always have your original driver's license with you whenever you drive. A copy is not good enough, so keep that at home.

Police

There are different classifications of police at Lakeside (in Mexico, actually). The *tránsitos* are considered the lowest level. They deal only with driving and traffic issues. They're real police, though, with real powers, although they're the least educated (often not having a high school education), and the least paid. The *tránsitos* often don't know the driving laws very well. In times

> *"Taking bribes is illegal in Mexico, so never offer it on your own."*

past, their salaries were kept low because the custom of taking *morditas* (bribes) made up for it. This practice is disappearing, but it still exists to some degree. And, expats are assumed to be rich, so we're the perfect targets.

Taking bribes is illegal in Mexico, so never offer it on your own. Your best bet, if you don't want to pay it, is to keep repeating, "*No hablo español*", or pretend you don't know what they're hinting at, or keep insisting that you want the ticket. Most of the time, the bribe will be more than the actual fine, so you're better off insisting on the ticket. Besides, if you pay the ticket within 10 days, the fine is cut in half. And remember, they cannot take any of your documents, including your license, under any circumstances.

There's a listing of Jalisco and federal driving laws in the Appendix. You'll want to keep a copy of them in your glove compartment to show the *tránsito* police what the law really says. If all else fails, call your lawyer's cell phone, whose number you should always have in your cell phone or on the Diving Accident Form in the Appendix. This will prevent the *tránsitos* from taking further advantage of you, if that's what they're trying to do.

> *"There's a listing of Jalisco and federal driving laws in the Appendix. You'll want to keep a copy of them in your glove compartment to show the tránsito police what the law really says."*

The next level up is the municipal police, called the *policía preventiva*. Their job is to prevent crime within their municipal area. Then there's the Jalisco state police force, which reports to the state governor. They're called *Policía Estatale*s. And then there are two classifications of federal police: the *Policía Federal*, and the *Policía Federal Ministerial*, whose job it is to conduct investigations. These levels are listed in increasing salary grade levels, so you're less likely to be approached for a *mordita* the higher up the ladder you go. And, lastly, there's the Mexican military, for very serious situations.

There are phone numbers in the Appendix for emergencies, and for reporting any police misconduct.

Passports

If you are an expat in Mexico, you should already have a passport from your home country. Mexico doesn't officially require one, but your home country will require one when/if you return. Plus, you will not be able to apply for an FM-2 or FM-3 visa without one, or open a bank account (in most banks), or get senior discount cards. And, you'll have trouble renting a house from a reputable agency, too, without one. Your passport is your primary form of identification here.

Because it's so important, you don't want to risk losing your passport by carrying it around with you every day. You'll want to have a certified copy made, which you can then keep in your car's glove compartment. Certified copies can only be made by a *Notario Público*. The place I recommend is Notaria 5. It's located in the orange stucco building at 245-D Hidalgo (that's the *carretera* – the main road) in Chapala. It's in the block just west of the main intersection of Hidalgo and Madero streets. They speak English, and are very easy to work with. The phone number is 376-765-2740.

If you need to renew, replace, or receive a new US passport, here is the US State Department link that can advise you about what you need in order to apply. http://tinyurl.com/54ay9.

And here is the link for Canadian expats: http://tinyurl.com/8nr6r59.

The closest US and Canadian consulates/embassies are in Guadalajara. Their locations are listed in the Appendix. A representative of the American Embassy comes to the Lake Chapala Society the first Wednesday of every month. You'll want to check the online schedule at: http://tinyurl.com/cutbbk8. A representative also visits the American Legion in Chapala. Their website is: www.americanlegionchapalapost7.org.

Appendix

Exploratory Trip Checklist

Planning your exploratory trip

☐ Make sure your passport is current.

☐ Book a flight to Guadalajara airport (5 – 7 day round trip).

☐ Book a bed and breakfast inn room in Ajijic.

During your exploratory trip

☐ Visit the Lake Chapala Society.

☐ Buy area maps.

☐ Decide whether you want to relocate to Lake Chapala.

☐ Find a place to live.

☐ Establish a mailing address for both envelopes and packages.

☐ Make arrangements for a border driver, if needed.

Move Planning Checklist

Four Weeks Before Moving

- ☐ Set a move date.

- ☐ Tell your family and friends.

- ☐ Decide what to do about your pets.

- ☐ Decide what to do about your house.

- ☐ Decide what to do about your car.

- ☐ Decide what to do about your belongings.

- ☐ Meet with accountant or financial advisor.

- ☐ Establish a banking plan.

- ☐ Establish new bank account/credit accounts, if needed.

- ☐ Extend your health insurance policy to 3 months past your planned move date.

- ☐ Get certified copies of your marriage license and other important documents, if applicable.

- ☐ Determine if your car insurance covers Mexico.

Appendix: Move Planning Checklist

Three Weeks Before Moving

- ☐ Pack the last 2 years of health records from your doctors and dentists.

- ☐ Switch all statements from hardcopy to online payment.

- ☐ Switch all periodicals from hardcopy to digital.

- ☐ Buy IKEA bags.

- ☐ Buy language translation applications and a GPS (with Mexican map) for portable electronic devices.

- ☐ Learn how your cell phone will behave, and how much it will cost to use in Mexico.

- ☐ Ship your books using M-Class.

Two Weeks Before Moving

- ☐ Pack 2 months of medication.

- ☐ Buy pet carriers.

- ☐ Make arrangements to pay all ongoing bills online.

- ☐ Notify your post office of your change of address.

- ☐ Pack a printout of the last 3 months of your primary checking account. You may not be able to access a printer quickly later.

- ☐ Pack three copies of all pages of your passport, your driver's license, your car's title, and your car's registration.

- ☐ If you are bringing pets, take them to the vet, and pack three copies of the international health certificate for each of them.

- ☐ Get a car checkup.

- ☐ Get a haircut.

One Week Before Moving

- ☐ Pack a copy of Jalisco and federal driving laws and fines in your car's glove compartment.

- ☐ Tell your bank and credit card companies that you're going to be in Mexico so they won't decline your "unusual location" transactions.

- ☐ If driving, bring 6,000 pesos for toll roads, gas, and lodging. Sometimes only cash is accepted, and/or your credit card may be declined due to "unusual location", even if you've notified them in advance.

- ☐ Make final border driver meeting arrangements.

Border Checklist

- ☐ Get an FMM tourist visa.

- ☐ Get a tourist vehicle permit and sticker.

- ☐ Pass customs.

- ☐ Purchase one month's auto insurance, if you don't already have Mexican auto insurance.

Moving In Checklist

First week

- ☐ Buy bottled water along with food.
- ☐ Get emergency numbers.
- ☐ Get locks changed.
- ☐ Determine household help names and schedules.
- ☐ Have existing electricity, gas, telephone, and tap water transferred to your name.
- ☐ Get TV service.
- ☐ Get internet service.
- ☐ Complete house walk-through with agency or landlord.
- ☐ Get name and phone number of handyman.
- ☐ Learn about the maintenance schedule of your gas tank, water tank, and cistern.
- ☐ Learn about garbage collection.
- ☐ Learn about fumigation.
- ☐ Join the Lake Chapala Society

Appendix: Moving In Checklist

- ☐ Buy several area maps. (glove compartment, purse, home)

- ☐ Make spare sets of keys.

- ☐ Choose mailing service.

Second week

- ☐ Apply for FM-2 or FM-3 visa status. You probably will not be able to open a Mexican bank account with an FMM card.

- ☐ Apply for Mexican health insurance.

- ☐ Make arrangements for a Mexican cell phone.

Third week

- ☐ Get new Mexican auto insurance.

- ☐ Arrange for household help, if needed.

Fourth week

- ☐ Upgrade your car's vehicle registration to correspond to your FM-3 or FM-2 status.

- ☐ Have important documents notarized.

- ☐ Get a DIF and an INAPAM discount card.

- ☐ Open a Mexican bank account.

Emergency Numbers and Words

Any emergency: **066**   (similar to 911)

24-Hour Ambulance: **065** (Red Cross)
- Red Cross   **376-765-2553, or 2308**
- Clinica Ajijic   **376-766-0622, or 0662**
- Clinica Maskaras (Riberas Del Pilar)   **3776-765-4838**
- Clinica Municipal (Chapala)   **376-765-5421**
- Clinica Municipal (Jocotepec)   **387-763-1920**

Police:
- Police – Chapala   **376-765-4444, or 2821**
- Police – Ajijic   **376-766-1760**
- Police – Jocotepec   **387-763-0006, or 0074**
- Police – Tránsito (Chapala)   **376-765-4747**

24-Hour Fire & Rescue :
- For all towns   **376-766-3615**

Road Service:
- Green Angels (Los Angeles Verde)   **078 or 800-903-9200**

Anonymous Crime Hotline 800-839-1416 (Routed via Canada, untraceable, and in English. For Lakeside crimes, suspicious activity, and police misconduct.)

Appendix: Emergency Numbers and Words

Common Emergency Words

do you speak English? = habla usted inglés?

I don't speak Spanish = no hablo español

the address is = la dirección es

my house = mi casa

I need = necesito

    police = policía

    firefighters = bomberos

    an ambulance = una ambulancia

    a doctor = un doctor

there is a = hay (pronounced "eye") un

man = hombre (om'-bre)

woman = mujer (moo-herr')

child = niño (boy), niña (girl)

traffic accident = accidente de tránsito

robber = ladrón

rapist = violador

fire = incendio

intruder = intruso

noise = ruido

gun = pistola

knife = cuchillo

very sick = muy enfermo

bleeding = hemorragia

people are hurt = personas son lastima

heart attack = ataque cardiac

no breathing = no respiración

death = muerte

come now, please = venir ahora, por favor

hurry = prisa

Appendix: Telephone Dialing

Telephone Dialing

- **Mexico's country code**
  - 52

- **Lakeside city codes**
  - 387 = municipality of Jocotepec, including Jocotepec and San Juan Cosalá
  - 376 = municipality of Chapala, including Chapala and Ajijic

- **To call a Mexican *land* phone from the same city code**
  - Dial only the 7-digit phone number

- **To call a Mexican *land* phone from a different city code**
  - 01 + city code + phone #

- **To call a Mexican *cell* phone from a *land* phone Lakeside**
  - 045 + city code + phone #

- **To call a Mexican *cell* phone from a *cell* phone Lakeside**
  - city code + phone #

- **To call the US or Canada**
  - 001 + area code + phone #

- **To call any other country**
    - 00 + country code + city code + phone #

- **To call US or Canadian toll-free numbers**
    - Instead of 800, dial 880
    - Instead of 866, dial 883
    - Instead of 877, dial 882
    - Instead of 888, dial 881

  These will <u>not</u> be free calls. They'll be charged at the international rate.

- **To call a Mexican *land* phone from the US or Canada**
    - 011 + 52 + city code + phone #

- **To call a Lakeside *cell* phone from the US**
    - 011 + 52 + 1 + 45 + 10-digit phone #

Web Boards, Forums, and Blogs

Web Boards and Forums
- http://tinyurl.com/846ruyg
    The most popular local web board.
- www.insidelakeside.com
    Another popular local web board.
- www.lakesidecrimetracker.com
    Tracks local crime incidents.
- http://tinyurl.com/9pgav4q
    A popular local forum.
- http://groups.yahoo.com/group/lakechapala/
    Lake Chapala Yahoo Group.

Blogs
- http://cookjmex.blogspot.mx
    Jim and Carol's blog.
- http://mexicodailyliving.blogspot.mx
    Patricia W.'s blog.
- http://boomerstomexico.com/
    Judy (Les) and David's blog.
- http://bigskysouthernsky.wordpress.com
    Mike and Barbara's blog.
- http://sietepuertas.wordpress.com
    Rob and Lynn's blog.

Recommended Reading

Magazines
- *El Ojo del Lago* (monthly – in English)
  Available free at local news stands.
  http://www.ojo.chapala.com
- *Lake Chapala Review* (monthly – in English)
  Available free at local news stands.
  www.lakechapalareview.com

Newspapers
- *Guadalajara Reporter* (weekly – in English)
  Available at local news stands – 15 pesos
  www.theguadalajarareporter.com
- *New York Times Sunday Edition*
  You can purchase this weekly at "Book Store" in Bugambilias Plaza, on the *carretera* in Ajijic at Calle Juan Alvarez cross street.

Books
- *Mexico's Lake Chapala & Ajijic: The Insider's Guide*
  Teresa A. Kendrik
  Mexico Traveler's Information, 2007
- *The Best How-To Book on Moving to Mexico*
  Carol Schmidt, Norma Hair, Rolly Brook
  Salsa Verde Press, 2009

Appendix: Recommended Reading

- *Live Better South of the Border: A Practical Guide to Living and Working*
    "Mexico" Mike Nelson
    Fulcrum Publishing, 2005
- *Midlife Mavericks: Women Reinventing Their Lives in Mexico*
    Karen Blue
    Universal Publishers, 2002
- *Mexico: Health and Safety Travel Guide*
    Robert H. Page, MD and Curtis P. Page, MD
    Medtogo, LLC, 2004
- *Head for Mexico – The Renegade Guide*
    Don Adams
    Trafford Publishing, 2006

Places and Services

The Lake Chapala Society, A.C.
16 de Septiembre #16-A
Ajijic, Jalisco
Phone: 376-766-1140
www.lakechapalasociety.com
Grounds open Monday – Saturday 9 to 5
Office open Monday – Saturday 10 to 2

U.S. Consulate General – Guadalajara
Progreso #175
Colonia Americana
C.P. 44100
Guadalajara, Jalisco
Phone: 333-268-2100
guadalajara.usconsulate.gov
Office open Monday - Friday 8 to 4:30

Consulate of Canada – Guadalajara
World Trade Center
Av. Mariano Otero #1249
Piso 8, Torre Pacífico
Col. Rinconada del Bosque
44530 Guadalajara, Jalisco
Phone: 333-671-4740
http://tinyurl.com/clt5op5
Office open Monday – Friday 10 to 2

Appendix: Places and Services

For visas and immigration
SEGOB (Secretaría de Gobernación) Inmigración
271 Hidalgo (*carretera*)
Chapala, Jalisco
www.inm.gob.mx
Office open Monday – Friday 9 to 1

For driver's license
Gobierno del Edo De Jalisco Sria. De Vialidad y Transporte
405 Flavio Romero de Velasco
Chapala, Jalisco
www.jalisco.gob.mx/wps/portal/sriaVialidad
Office open Monday – Friday 9 to 2

For DIF and INAPAM cards
DIF/INAPAM Office
Degollado #327, Chapala
Phone: 376-765-3349
web.dif.gob.mx   www.inapam.gob.mx
Office open Monday – Tuesday 9 to 2

For taxis
Ajijic taxi stand (sitio) at Plaza
376-766-0674 or 766-1663
7am. to 8pm

Chapala taxi stand (sitio) at Plaza
376-765-3511 or 765-4697
6am to 9pm

Jalisco Driving Laws and Fines

Jalisco's Traffic Laws in Spanish
http://tinyurl.com/8k66xxy

Jalisco's Traffic Laws Translated
The following legal translations are kindly provided by Lic. Spencer McMullen, Chapala (attorney and official court translator). Not all of Jalisco's driving laws and fines are presented here – just the ones most likely to be of interest to new expats.

Fines
Traffic fines are calculated as multiples of Jalisco's minimum *daily* wage, which in 2012 is 60.57 pesos (approximately $4.55 USD).

Regulation Article 180 states that if the fine is paid within 10 working days, you will get a 50% discount. If it is paid within 29 working days, you will get a 25% discount.

Fines are paid at the *Hacienda* (Treasury) office at:

> Hacienda
> Degollado #306
> Chapala, Jalisco

Fines can also be paid at most banks, as well as 7-Eleven and OXXO convenience stores after filling out and

Appendix: Jalisco Driving Laws and Fines

bringing the form on the following website: http://tinyurl.com/8c5c4hf.

If the fine is from federal police, rather than tránsito police, it can be paid at any Bancomer bank office, or online at: http://tinyurl.com/9zramlu.

Fines are levied against a car rather than a person. If someone else drives your car and is given a fine, and if he/she doesn't pay the fine, you will have to pay it when you renew your car's registration.

Insurance

The state of Jalisco requires that all vehicles (including drivers and passengers) be insured (Article 53 and 167-bis) for 6,000 days minimum wage (360,000 pesos). For motorcycles 125cc and over, the amount is 2,000 days minimum wage (120,000 pesos) (Article 57).

Rules for Police Officers

Police officers in Jalisco **may not** **take your driver's license** or any other document, except in the case of public transport drivers. This is not the case in some other Mexican states.

Article 159: The traffic authorities are not authorized to take from the driver his/her license, permission, identification, registration card, or any other document, with the exception of public transportation vehicles transporting passengers or cargo.

Police officers *may not* **commit extortion** (ask for bribes, or *morditas*).

Article 189: He who commits the act of extortion, who, by means of duress, demands that another give, send, or deposit for his benefit or the benefit of a third party, things, money, or documents where there are legal consequences. The same crime is committed when, under duress, one is obligated to sign or destroy a document contains obligations, or about a debt. If the extortioner achieves his goal, then 1 to 9 years of prison will be imposed. If the extortioner does not achieve his goal, then 6 months to 6 years of prison will be imposed. When the means of duress is the temporary detainment of a person to demand things, money, or documents, or certain acts that affect the wealth of the victim, the penalty will be from 10 to 30 years of prison, and a fine of 500 days of minimum daily wage (3,000 pesos), even if the extortioner isn't successful.

Article 146 (Abuse of Authority – all public persons who exceed their authority) also relates to the payment of bribes.
III. When the person improperly slows down or denies private parties the protection or service that they have the obligation to give, or impeding the process of applying for a service.
IV. When the person does an act, or authorizes or permits an act undermining the rights guaranteed by the Constitution of the United States of Mexico or of the State.
VIII. When one is made to give money or other things of value that doesn't belong to the other person.

Appendix: Jalisco Driving Laws and Fines

He who commits the act of Abuse of Authority will receive the following penalty. If the amount of economic benefit by his acts doesn't exceed 196 days minimum wage, one to five years in prison will be imposed, as well as a fine of 20 days minimum wage.

Regarding authorities **stopping and impounding your car**:

Article 49: Any vehicle registered in the State or in another federal entity can drive freely, and traffic officials cannot interrupt or stop the driving of any vehicle, except in cases of flagrant infractions, or in the application of a security measure expressly provided for in this ordinance.

Article 70: The State and municipal traffic authorities, in conformity with the norms of the traffic regulations, and as a security measure, will impound vehicles in the cases in conformity with the procedure established under this law.

Article 156: Vehicles will be impounded as a measure of protection in the following cases.
I. When driving without license plates or permission to be on the road.
II. The vehicle has plates placed over the real plates.
III. The vehicle lacks necessary equipment to be on the road, or is being used inconsistent with its permission to be on the road.
IV. The vehicle is in a prohibited place, blocking a garage or reserved parking space, or abandoned on a public right-

of-way, or it blocks traffic or pedestrians without the driver being there.

V. Reoffenders that continue to contaminate.

VI. A private car that is painted or colored to look like a police car or traffic officer car or public transport.

Article 158: The traffic authorities, as a security measure, can impound a vehicle against the will of the driver or owner in the following situations.

I. Where the vehicle is used when the driver is committing a crime.

II. When there is an official report of the vehicle being used in a crime.

III. Per court order.

IV. Violation by the driver of the prior articles

V. For violations of Article 156 part I, II, and III of this code.

Article 167: Impoundable offenses:

I. Not having the sticker (one with license number) matching plates on car.

III. Driving without license plates or with expired plates.

IV. Improper use of novelty license plates.

Article 50: When there is an accident and people are injured, or one of the drivers is under the influence of alcohol, or there is damage to government property, whether municipal, state or federal, the proper authorities should immediately proceed to secure the vehicles and send

Appendix: Jalisco Driving Laws and Fines

them to the public towing yard, and the drivers to the proper judicial authority corresponding to the matter.

Authorities *may not* impound a vehicle for any other reason than those listed above.

Complaints

If you have a complaint against *any public official* (including any police officer), use the form located here: http://tinyurl.com/8jbrl6d. Make a copy of this form, and keep it in your car so you know what information to collect, and so an offending police officer can see that you're planning to file a report. The form can be submitted to any federal government office. If it's serious offense, you may want to seek the advice of an attorney to make sure the complaint gets attention and resolution.

Driving

If you **drive someone else's car**, and the owner isn't in it, you will need a signed letter from the owner authorizing you to drive it, plus a copy of their ID, in order to compare signatures.

Article 72: Vehicles not registered in the state and that remain in the state for more than 6 continuous months ought to satisfy the requirements of this law and ordinance. If the time in the state is less than 6 months, then the vehicle only needs to comply with the requirements of the state it's from. *(This appears to apply only to equipment requirements.)*

Article 161: The following infractions will be **fined 1 day's minimum wage (60 pesos).**

I. Lack of bumpers/fenders.

II. Lack of windshield wipers.

III. Lack of side mirrors.

IV. Lack of protective equipment mention in these regulations.

V. Failing to present current registration (*tarjeta de circulación*).

VI. Having a damaged/smashed windshield that obstructs visibility.

VII. Failing to have the sticker which has the license plate number on it.

VIII. Using lights not permitted.

IX. Throwing any type of article out of the vehicle, or placing anything in the roadway that would impede driving, parking, or stopping of vehicles.

Article 162: The following infractions will be **fined 1 day's minimum wage (60 pesos).**

I. Not presenting your driver's license. (*Note: must be the original; not a copy.*)

II. Parking in a prohibited spot on a local street.

III. Lights not working.

IV. Using glass, or anything else, that totally impedes visibility into the vehicle.

V. Repealed.

VI. Parking the wrong way on a street.

VII. Repealed.

VIII. Driving in reverse more than 10 meters.

Appendix: Jalisco Driving Laws and Fines

IX. Making a prohibited turn.
X. Making excessive noise with the horn or muffler.
XI. Having a missing license plate.

Article 163: The following infractions will be **fined 2 days minimum wage (120 pesos)**.

I. Doing auto repair on the highway when it obstructs or blocks traffic, except in cases of emergency.
II. Abandoning a vehicle on a public right-of-way per the statute.
III. Loading and unloading outside of authorized times.
IV. Driving your vehicle with people, pets, or objects obstructing your driving.
V. Placing your license plate on other than required in the code.
VI. Driving a vehicle that the transit authorities have declared out of circulation.
VII. Failing to comply with an order to take a vehicle off the road.
VIII. Driving with license plates covered or obstructed, totally or partially, or using other plates with numbers that impair vision of the proper plates.
IX. Parking in a space reserved for handicapped people.
X. Modifying the characteristics of a vehicle without authorization.
XI. Transporting cargo in a manner other than provided for in the ordinance.
XII. Failing to obey the instructions of a traffic officer.
XIII. Driving in a pedestrian zone.
XIV. Failing to stop for a railroad crossing.

XV. Parking where it blocks a garage or other reserved parking.
XVI. Transporting heavy machinery or equipment without the corresponding permission.
XVII. Repealed.

Article 164: The following infractions will be **fined 3 days minimum wage (180 pesos)**.
I. Repealed.
II. Repealed.
III. Not notifying the government of the sale of the vehicle, or change of address of the owner.
IV. Transporting people in cargo vehicles without proper protection.
V. Repealed.
VI. Allowing unlicensed, or person without a valid license, to drive your vehicle.
VII. Driving a vehicle requiring a specific license, and not showing it.
VIII. Driving on the sidewalk or parking on it in a manner that, or during times that, impedes safe pedestrian movement.
IX. Driving a motor vehicle, being a minor, and not having the proper permission per Article 62.
X. Driving in prohibited zones of *calzadas* (roads), *avenidas* (avenues), traffic stopping areas, highways, in restricted parking zones on the days and times the signs say, or with a yellow curb.
XI. Not visibly showing an operator's or driver's identification card *(appears to apply to bus drivers)*.

Appendix: Jalisco Driving Laws and Fines

XII. Carrying excess passengers in a public transit vehicle per specifications.

XIII. Loading and unloading passengers in zones not authorized.

XIV. Driving with doors open.

XV. Repealed.

XVI. Repealed.

XVII. Hurling insults at traffic officers, if it can be proved.

XVIII. Passing on the right.

XIX. Changing lanes without caution.

XX. Driving a vehicle on bike paths, pedestrian zones, plazas, and trails for exclusive use of pedestrians without authority from the competent authority.

XXI. Driving a vehicle using a cell phone, except when it has hands-free equipment.

XXII. Motorcyclists who do not respect their driving lane in violation of the law and these regulations.

Article 165: The following infractions will be **fined 8 days minimum wage (484 pesos).**

Running a red light, or failing to stop when instructed for a traffic officer.

Article 166: The following infractions will be **fined 8 days minimum wage (180 pesos).**

I. Driving with no lights.

II. Repealed.

III. Repealed.

IV. Repealed.

V. Moving from the scene of an accident, except when the parties have come to an agreement, or per the instructions of a traffic officer.

VI. Repealed.

Article 146: The following infractions will be subject to a **fine of 10 days minimum wage** (600 pesos), as well as subject the vehicle to being impounded in the event of violating parts I, III, or IV.

I. Not having the sticker (one with license number) matching plates on car.

II. Repealed.

III. Driving without license plates or with expired plates.

IV. Improper use of novelty license plates.

V. Impeding, or not allowing, emergency or police vehicles to pass when they have their emergency lights and siren on; or driving close behind them to take advantage of that circumstance.

VI. Repealed.

VII. A driver that drives the wrong way, or unjustifiably invades the opposing lane to pass on two-way highways in urban zones.

Article 167: The following infractions will be subject to a **fine of 10 days minimum wage** (600 pesos).

I. Not having the car's license sticker number match the plates.

II. Repealed.

III. Driving without plates, or with expired plates.

IV. Improper use of special or vanity plates.

Appendix: Jalisco Driving Laws and Fines

V. Impeding the passage of emergency vehicles when they are using lights and sirens, or driving right behind them, taking advantage of others moving out of the way.

VI. Repealed.

VII. Driving the wrong way, or unjustifiably invading the opposite lane to pass on highways in urban zones.

Article 167-bis: The following infractions will be subject to a **fine of 10 to 30 days minimum wag**e (600 to 1,800 pesos).

I. Not using a seatbelt or using it inadequately, the driver s well as the other passengers.

II. Transporting a child under 12 years old in the front seats, except vehicles that have no rear seats. In both cases, the child should be transported in security seats, and with a proper restraint system adequate for their age, and built duly secured.

III. The driver of a vehicle who exceeds the maximum permitted speed limit by 10 kilometers per hour whenever the speed limit is posted. In those zones where speed is expressly restricted, such as school zones and hospital zones, the regulations point out the maximum speed limits in those areas as well as other areas. In these cases, there is no tolerance, and in no manner is exceeding the speed limit permitted.

IV. Not having insurance covering damages to third parties. This fine will be extinguished if, within 20 business days of the infraction, a third party liability policy is shown to the executive branch transit department which complies with the regulations of the transit law of the State of Jalisco.

Apart from third party liability insurance, vehicle liability coverage that offers towing service shall have insurance to pay for damages that towed vehicles may suffer.

Article 167-ter: The following infractions will be subject to a **fine of 10 to 20 days minimum wag**e (600 to 1,200 pesos) for motorcyclists of any type of motorcycle, 3-wheel cycle, quad or motorcar, when driving.
I. Not properly wearing, and adjusted with straps, a protective helmet for motorcyclists, and, when applicable, for their passenger.
II. Carrying a passenger who is a minor who cannot hold on themselves and reach the foot pegs.
III. When exceeding the number of passengers on the driving card.
IV. Not driving in compliance with the regulations of this present law.
V. Apart from the prior mentioned sanctions, in the event of repeated offenses, the unit will be taken off the streets as a means of safety.

Article 168 states that all Jalisco-plated vehicles (not foreign-plated vehicles) must have a smog sticker. If not, there will be a **fine of 20 days minimum wage (120,000 pesos)**. But, that fine will be waived if the vehicle is in compliance within 15 business days of receiving the citation. The same holds true for a vehicle visibly contaminating the atmosphere.

Appendix: Jalisco Driving Laws and Fines

Article 168-bis: He who commits the infraction of driving a motor vehicle where it is detected that the driver has 50 to 80 milligrams per 100 milliliters of alcohol in his blood (or .25 to .40 milligrams of alcohol per liter of air breathed out), or is under the influence of drugs, when committing any other infraction will be **fined 150 to 200 days minimum wage (9,000 to 12,000 pesos)**. In this case, the driver will be subject to an alcohol breath test. If the driver refuses the test, he will be sent to the Ministerio Publico, and they will do a medical test (draw blood). The **driver's license will be suspended** per the terms of the third paragraph of Article 170 of these regulations.

Article 122: The driver who drives a motor vehicle, and more than 130 milligrams per 100 milliliters of alcohol is detected in the blood, or over .65 milligrams of alcohol per liter of air breathed out, or under the influence of drugs that alter the ability to drive when committing another infraction applicable to the driving laws will be **fined 150 to 200 days minimum wage (9,000 to 12,000 pesos), 60 to 120 days community service, and a 3 month driver's license suspension.**

If the driver has more than 150 milligrams per 100 milliliters of alcohol in his blood, he will **placed at the disposition of the Ministerio Publico** with the appropriate legal consequences.

Article 166-bis: He who commits the infraction of parking in or driving in the exclusive public transportation lanes will be fined **200 to 400 days minimum wages (12,114 to 24,228 pesos).** *This is between approximately $1,000 to $2,000 UDS dollars, so this is very serious. The transportation lanes referred to are the macrobus lanes in the middle of main streets, like Independencía, in Guadalajara. People making illegal left turns and traversing the lanes can also be fined.*

Article 170: In the event another violation of the law is committed within 3 months, the amount of the **fine will be doubled.** In the event another violation of Article 167 sections VI or VII is committed within 30 days, the violator will have the **choice of being arrested for 12 hours or doing 2 days of community service**. In the event another violation of Article 168-bis is committed within 60 days, the violator will also be punished with a 12 to 36 hour mandatory arrest. If there is a further violation within 30 days, apart from the administrative arrest, the driver will have their **driver's license cancelled**, and will have to apply for a **new license after waiting for 1 year**, and after **toxicological and alcohol examinations** demonstrate that the person isn't an alcoholic or addicted to drugs.

Accidents

Article 50: When there is an accident and people are injured, or one of the drivers is under the influence of alcohol, or there is damage to government property, whether municipal, state or federal, the proper authorities should immediately proceed to **secure the vehicles and**

send them to the public towing yard, and the **drivers to the proper judicial authority** corresponding to the matter.

Article 51: After an accident when there are only material damages between the parties involved or third parties, and there are no injuries or any deaths, and if the drivers have all their documents in order, the parties can agree to settle the matter amongst themselves and **make and sign an agreement**. In this instance, the vehicles will not be towed, nor will citations be issued for infractions except infractions committed separately or independently from the accident.

Federal Driving Laws and Fines

Mexico's Traffic Laws in Spanish
http://tinyurl.com/8ukg5ce

Mexico's Traffic Laws Translated
The following legal translations are kindly provided by Lic. Spencer McMullen, Chapala (attorney and official court translator). Not all of Mexico's driving laws and fines are presented here – just the ones most likely to be of interest to new expats.

Article 38: When the owner of a **vehicle transfers** the vehicle to another party, they will still be liable for infractions until they give proper notice of transfer to the authorities. The registration will expire upon transfer to another party, and the new party will have to apply for and obtain the new registration papers before operating, or permitting another to operate, the vehicle. The fine is up to 5 days minimum wage (300 pesos).

Article 46: Private vehicles from outside the country **may drive on federal highways** in accordance with international treaties and agreements approved by the Senate and published in the Federal register, or in the event that such doesn't exist, as long as such driving doesn't contradict these regulations.

Appendix: Federal Driving Laws and Fines

Article 66: It is prohibited **to leave or throw trash**, bottle, glass, nails, wire, or any other material that can cause damage to people or vehicles using the roadway. Anyone removing a vehicle after an accident should **clean the roadway** of glass and other material that has fallen onto it. The fine is up to 30 days minimum wage (1800 pesos).

Article 79: To drive a motor vehicle, it is necessary to be in **full control of your faculties**, both mental and physical, carry a **valid driver's license** or other document that authorizes you to drive the vehicle. The fine is up to 30 days minimum wage (1800 pesos).

Likewise, to operate or drive a motor vehicle, the **driver needs to use their seatbelt**. The fines are: 1st offense 2 days minimum wage, 2nd offense 4 days, 3rd offense 6 days (120, 240, and 360 pesos, respectively).

Article 99: Vehicles should **drive on the right side** of the roadway, except under the following circumstances. The fine is up to 20 days minimum wage (1200 pesos).

- When passing another vehicle.
- When the road isn't large enough for 2 lanes.
- When there are obstructions on the right half, and it is necessary to drive on the left. In this case, drivers should yield to vehicles coming from the opposite direction, moving to an unobstructed part.

- When the road is divided into 3 lanes for traffic in both directions, vehicles should be driven to the **extreme right lane**.

Article 80: For a vehicle to drive on public highways, it is required to have proper and clearly legible **registration** issued by the proper authority. The fine is up to 30 days minimum wage (1800 pesos).

Article 100: When the driver of a vehicle is driving on a 2-lane highway with traffic moving in both directions, the driver should **drive on the extreme right** when encountering an oncoming vehicle. The fine is up to 5 days minimum wage (300 pesos).

Article 118: **Speed limits** when not indicated by signs are the following in kilometers per hour. The fine is up to 10 days minimum wage (600 pesos).

Speed limit for vehicles with a net weight no greater than 3,500 kgs.

In urban zones – 50km/hour
In rural zones (daytime) – 100km/hour
In rural zones (nighttime) – 90km/hour

Article 119: Notwithstanding the speed limits in the prior article, or those indicated by signage, **speed should take into account** driving conditions, the road, visibility, the vehicle, and the driver. A driver also shouldn't drive at such a **slow speed** that he interrupts traffic, except when

Appendix: Federal Driving Laws and Fines

necessary due to security reasons, or compliance with the law, or any other justified cause. Drivers are **prohibited from speed exhibitions** or races on public highways. The fine is up to 10 days minimum wage (600 pesos).

Article 147: Except regarding the competent authority, whoever, without authorization of the holder, **retains documentation** that proves identity or the immigration status of a foreigner in the country, will be fined from 1,000 to 10,000 minimum wage days. ***This is a fine of 62,330 to 623,300 pesos, or $4,721 USD to $47,210 USD. This is worth remembering. No one in Mexico can legally take your driver's license, passport, tourist card, or visa unless specifically authorized.***

Article 183: The driver of a vehicle involved in an accident where there is injury or death or damage to the vehicles or other property should immediately **stop at the scene of the accident**, or as close as possible, and remain there until the arrival of the proper authorities. The fine is up to 50 days minimum wage (3000 pesos).

The driver should **stop without posing a danger** to other drivers, and place warning devices. The fine is up to 20 days minimum wage (1200 pesos).

Article 184: The driver of a vehicle involved in an accident where somebody is injured shall proceed to give help to others, if possible, within their means, to **transport the injured** parties in their own vehicle to the nearest location where they can receive assistance. The fine is up to 50 days minimum wage (3000 pesos).

In all cases where one involved in an accident has left the scene of the accident to look for help for the victims, they are obligated to **return to the scene** of the accident and place themselves at the disposal of the authority investigating the accident. The fine is up to 50 days minimum wage (3000 pesos).

The drivers of other vehicles that pass the accident scene are **obligated to stop and to aid** in the help of the injured parties. The obligation is the same if the people arrive at the accident scene driving, walking, or as a passenger.

Article 185: If, as a result of an accident, there is not injury or death, and there is only material damage, the parties may **make an agreement** to resolve the issue without involving the traffic authorities. The agreement should list the names of the parties, their addresses, license plate numbers, and the date and place of the accident. This does not apply to damages to national property, or to federal public service vehicles.

Article 186: The traffic authorities can request that a driver of a vehicle involved in an accident make a **voluntary written report** of the accident.

Article 187: Any person who provides information to the traffic authorities in relation to an accident, and is **not**

Appendix: Federal Driving Laws and Fines

truthful, will be subject to penalties pursuant to criminal law.

Article 190: The Secretary shall keep an individual **registry of each driver**, noting judicial rulings that affect their ability to drive, as well as accidents they have been involved in.

Article 191: The Secretary of Communications and Transportation shall keep an individual **registry of every driver's traffic infractions** committed, at the discretion of the Secretary, as deserved.

Article 194: The federal traffic authorities should immediately detain any driver **under the influence of alcoholic beverages or drugs,** and take them to the nearest doctor for an examination to determine their mental state for the fine to be imposed and to be turned over to the prosecutor's office.

Article 197: The infractions and regulations under this code shall be **enforced by the federal transit authorities**, with tickets approved by the Secretary of Communications and Transportation.

The **original and a copy** shall be given to the offender. The first will be a receipt for the document taken as a guarantee for payment for a term of 50 days, and the copy as a notice to appear for the offender to pay the corresponding fine.

The offender has the right to have the ticket **assigned** to the federal **police office closest to him**.

If 30 working days from the date of infraction have passed, and the ticket has not been paid, **collection will be assigned** to the state or federal treasury department.

Fines may be appealed by the offender, or duly authorized legal representative, within 15 working days, starting the day after the offense. The writing must be directed to the Director General of Legal Affairs, or to the Director General of the central SCT in whose jurisdiction the offense was committed. The offender must **send a copy of their disagreement** to the office in the jurisdiction of the offense.

The written disagreement should **offer evidence, and put forward the defenses** that the offender considers necessary as it relates to the offense that are a basis for his claim. In light of the evidence and defenses presented, the Director General of Legal Affairs or the Director General of the SCT will have 30 days to resolve the matter.

Article 200-9: If there is an accident as a result of the infractions of these regulations, the **fine for the offense will be doubled**.

Article 200-10: Offenders of Articles 79 Paragraph 1 and Article 80, who, after the fact, **can provide the documentation**, will be fined 15 days minimum wage (900 pesos), instead of the fine that corresponds to not having

Appendix: Federal Driving Laws and Fines

said documents. The same fine will apply to those who didn't show a valid driver's license.

Article 200-11: Offenses committed by **passengers or pedestrians** will be admonished by the corresponding transit authority.

Article 200-12: Any other infraction of these regulations not specified in Article 200 will be fined **up to 50 days minimum wage**, at the discretion of the Secretary of Communications and Transportation.

Article 201: Fines for **committing the same infraction** may be up to double those indicated at the discretion of the Secretary of Communications and Transportation.

Article 202: If the fine isn't paid within 15 days of the offense, the **fine will increase 50%.**

Article 203: When a ticket is for multiple offenses, the **fines are cumulative**.

Article 204: **Owners of vehicles are solely responsible** for the drivers of those vehicles, and for the payment of fines for violations of these regulations.

Federal Penal Code: Capitulo III – **Abuse of Authority**: *This code is very similar to the State of Jalisco abuse of authority code.*

Vehicle Accident Form

Fill in the blanks regarding your relevant information so that it is available if you have an accident. Make sure you have a copy of this in your car – or have a copy of this book – so you can also see the various laws that might apply to your situation, as well as phone numbers of people who can help you.

**Emergency hotline – Lake Chapala area
(Police, Fire, Ambulance)**   **066**

Green Angels (assistance on toll highways)   078

My Mexican telephone numbers:
Home   _____
Cell   _____

Attorney
Name: _____
Telephones:
Office: _____
Cell: _____

My insurance adjuster: (At least a telephone #)
_____
_____

My vehicle insurance agent:
_____

Appendix: Vehicle Accident Form

Name of insurance company: _____
Policy number: _____
Emergency contacts:
    Local (neighbor or friend)
    Name: _____
    Telephone: _____
    Cell: _____

    Family contact #1:
    Name: _____
    Relationship: _____
    Country: _____
    Country telephone code: _____
    Telephone: _____
    Cell: _____

    Family contact #2:
    Name: _____
    Relationship: _____
    Country: _____
    Country telephone code: _____
    Telephone: _____
    Cell: _____

At the site of the accident, fill out this form, and keep it.

Date:_____
Time:_____

Road conditions:
_____

Traffic conditions:
_____

Weather conditions:
_____

Visibility:
_____

Your vehicle:
Driver's name: _____
Driver's license number:_____ issued by the state/province of
_____
Country_____
Vehicle license plate number:_____ Issued by the state/province of
_____
Country_____
Vehicle make:_____
Model:_____
Year_____

Appendix: Vehicle Accident Form

Other vehicle(s):
Owner's name: _____

Owner's address: _____
_____
_____

Owner's telephone number: _____

Driver's name: _____

Driver's address: _____
_____
_____

Driver's telephone number: _____

Driver's license number: _____
issued by the State/province of
_____
Country_____
Owner's insurance company, policy number and contact information: _____
_____
_____

Vehicle license plate number: _____
Issued by the state of: _____
Country: _____

Vehicle make:_____
Model:_____
Year:_____
Witnesses' information:
Names: Telephone numbers:
_____
_____
_____
_____
_____
_____
_____
_____

Details of the Accident

Record as much detail as possible: Direction of travel of your vehicle and the other vehicle(s), speeds, color of traffic light, road signs, statements made by other driver, statements made by witnesses.

_____
_____
_____
_____
_____
_____
_____
_____
_____
_____

Appendix: Vehicle Accident Form

Appendix: Vehicle Accident Form

Use this road diagram to describe the directions of travel and the positions of vehicles after the accident. Where appropriate, write in the names of the streets. Mark an "N" for North on the compass star as an aid to orienting the accident scene.

Questions to ask (in English and Spanish):

Please, I need some information from you. *Por favor, necesito información de usted.*

Driver's name. *Nombre del conductor.*
Driver's address. *La dirección del conductor*
Driver's telephone number. *El numero de teléfono del conductor.*
Driver's license information. *Información de la licencia de conductor.*
    Number. *Numero*
    Issued by the State of *De que estado es su licencia*
    Country. *De que pais es su licencia*

Owner of vehicle (from registration). *Datos del dueno del vehiculo:*
    Name. *Nombre*
    Address. *Dirección*
    Telephone number. *Numero de teléfono*
    Owner's insurance information. *Información del seguro*
    Company name. *Nombre de la compania*
    Company address. *Dirección de la compania*
    Policy number. *Numero de la poliza*
    Contact information. *Información del contacto*

Appendix: Common Conversions

Common Conversions

Measurements in Mexico are in metrics.

Outside
Temperature is measured on the Celsius scale:
- Fahrenheit = Centigrade x 1.8 + 32
- Centigrade = (Fahrenheit – 32)/1.8
- Example: 72°F = 22°C

Distance: A kilometer is longer than a mile.
- Kilometer = .6 miles (approx.)
- Mile = 1.6 kilometers (approx.)
- Speed (example): 40 kilometers/hour = 64 miles/hour

Inside
Oven temperature
- 325°F = 163°C
- 350°F = 177°C
- 375°F = 191°C
- 400°F = 204°C
- 425°F = 218°C
- 450°F = 232°C
- 475°F = 246°C

Weight
- Ounce = 28.4 grams
- Gram = .04 ounce
- Kilogram = 2.2 pounds
- Pound = .5 kg

Volume
- The Spanish word for teaspoon is *cucharadita,* and it's the same size.
- The Spanish word for tablespoon is *cuchara*, and it's the same size.
- The Spanish word for cup is *taza,* and it's the same size.
- A liter is a little bigger than a quart.
- Quart = .95 liter
- Liter = 1.1 quarts
- Gallon = 4.54 liters
- 5 liters = 1.4 gallons
- 20 liters (size of standard water *garrafón*) = 5.6 gallons

Length
- Inch = 2.54 centimeters
- Centimeter = .4 inch
- Foot = .3 meter
- A meter is 3 inches longer than a yard
- Yard = .9 meter
- Meter = 1.1 yard

Index

Abogados...*See* Lawyers (Abogados)
Ajijic...22, 125, 126, 127, 131, 146, 148, 158, 165, 166, 170, 174, 177, 178, 181, 182, 192, 208, 211, 241, 256
Aljibe...*See* Water:Cistern (Aljibe)
Apostilles - Certified Documents..................69, 70
Appendix............................249
ATM Machines...24, 65, 66, 116, 234, 235
Auctions..............59, 60, 61, 62
Baking................................209
Banking...27, 47, 63, 65, 66, 67, 72, 80, 82, 83, 88, 110, 116, 231, 233, 234, 235, 238, 243, 247
Beauty Salons and Barbers 212
Bicycles..............................151
Blogs..................................261
Book Store.........................181
Books.................................262
Border Driver...34, 76, 83, 92, 96, 252
Bribes..................*See* Morditas
Bus...34, 107, 116, 146, 147, 180, 241
Car Insurance...68, 91, 94, 112, 113, 144, 155, 157, 158
Chapala.......124, 125, 128, 146
Checklists
    Border.............................253
    Exploratory Trip.............249
    Move Planning................250
    Moving In........................254

Climate.........57, 118, 119, 209
CONDUSEF.......................235
Conversions................299, 300
Cooking.............................209
Credit Rating
    Mexican.................233, 234
    US........................29, 47, 49
Crime...19, 42, 43, 82, 188, 189, 246, 270
Crime Hotline...................256
Cruz Roja...*See* Red Cross (Cruz Roja)
Customs (Aduana)...45, 46, 56, 90, 93, 94, 95, 114, 115, 116, 210, 211
DEET.................................185
Dentists........................71, 195
DIF...116, 147, 194, 238, 241, 242, 265
Driver's License...80, 92, 115, 151, 152, 243, 244, 245, 265, 267, 272, 279, 280, 283, 285, 289
Driving Laws...81, 245, 246, 266, 282
    Federal............................282
    Jalisco.............................266
DVDs..............55, 76, 165, 222
DVRs...................................55
eBay......................59, 183, 210
Electricity...102, 184, 214, 216, 218
Embassy
    American.................248, 264
    Canada............................264
    Mexican..........................238
Emergency Numbers..........256

Emergency Words..............257
Expats
   Number of........................14
Exploratory Trip
   Reasons for 20
Flea Markets ....*See* Tianguis
Florida 14
FMM Tourist Card...38, 90, 91, 92, 93, 110, 162, 236, 237, 239, 285
Forums 261
Fumigation - Extermination 106
Galeria Mall 148, 179
Garbage Collection 105, 212
Gardeners...*See* Housekeepers - Gardeners
Garrafóns 168, 169, 170
Gas 102, 104, 214
Gasoline 88, 89, 97, 153
   Cost of......................88, 153
GPS 75, 96
Green Angels................97, 256
Guadalajara...19, 21, 24, 114, 120, 123, 128, 130, 132, 146, 148, 157, 163, 178, 180, 181, 183, 185, 191, 196, 224, 241, 248, 280
Hacienda 51, 93, 159, 266
Health Care
   Cost of......19, 111, 190, 192
   Quality of.......................191
Health Insurance...68, 72, 111, 112, 200, 201
   IMSS...196, 197, 198, 199, 200, 238
   Private 68, 71, 111, 200
   Seguro Popular.......199, 238
Housekeepers - Gardeners...31, 102, 113, 142, 202, 203, 205
   Christmas Bonus (Aguinaldo) 204

Cost of...........................205
IFE voting credential 207
IKEA Bags 73, 167
Immigration
   SEGOB INM .240, 241, 265
INAPAM...116, 194, 238, 241, 242, 265
Income
   Income Needed...14, 18, 39, 238, 240
Internet...18, 20, 43, 53, 63, 75, 80, 87, 103, 134, 135, 219, 220, 221, 222, 223, 224, 226, 230
IPAB...................................235
Jocotepec...124, 130, 131, 146, 156, 256
Juries 122
Keys76, 83, 102, 108, 177, 205
Lake Chapala Society...25, 106, 107, 108, 126, 132, 136, 137, 148, 149, 176, 178, 180, 206, 210, 248, 264
Language
   Instruction 136, 137, 182
   Translation Applications...75, 134
Lawyers (Abogados)...114, 120, 121, 238
Libel - Slander...................122
López Mateos Stores 178
Magazines 262
Mail...33, 34, 58, 109, 183, 184, 209, 210, 211
Maps...25, 75, 96, 101, 107, 151, 181
Medicare...68, 190, 191, 197, 201
Medications...77, 82, 192, 193, 194, 199
Morditas 114, 245, 246, 268

Index

Motorcycles...50, 157, 159, 160, 244, 278
Move
   Cost Of 38
Moving Companies 54
Names 31, 32, 91
Negotiating Prices...141, 142, 167
Newspapers 262
Notaria Pública...27, 115, 152, 247
Notario Público...27, 115, 120, 247
Nurseries (*viveros*) 182
Passport...21, 29, 31, 80, 91, 92, 95, 116, 121, 162, 179, 242, 243, 247, 285
PayPal 176, 231
Pets...31, 34, 44, 45, 46, 61, 77, 83, 86, 87, 88, 95, 107, 151, 207, 208, 273
   Birds 45
   Carriers 77
   Cats 45, 77, 87
   Grooming 44, 208
   Horses 46
   International Health Certificates 78, 80, 83, 95
   Motel 6 87
   Quarantines 45, 46
   Renting With 31
   Vaccinations 78
   Veterinarians 44, 208
Phones
   Cell...74, 76, 86, 108, 111, 150, 155, 219, 227, 228, 229, 230, 235, 275
   Land 55, 103, 219, 227
   Smart 230
Places 264
Police...43, 68, 81, 96, 114, 121, 131, 150, 154, 155, 156, 161, 188, 245, 246, 247, 267, 270, 271, 276, 288
Politics 122
PROFECO 186, 218
Radio 223
Real Estate
   Governing Organizaions...26, 27
   Multiple Listing Service (MLS) 20
   Recommended Reading 262
Red Cross (Cruz Roja)...148, 154, 176, 195, 196
Rental Agencies 22, 30, 31, 104
Rental Cars 23, 24, 143, 144
Renting
   Reasons For 27
Rosetta Stone Language Course 21, 137
Sales Tax 50, 51, 230
San Antonio...125, 128, 146, 164, 174, 211, 220
San Juan Cosalá 130, 131
Sandi Books 181
Services 264
Social Security .18, 66, 80, 238
Solar Energy 218
Spanish Dictionary 73, 134
Spencer McMullen...121, 156, 160, 266, 282
Tablets 219, 230
Taxis 24, 145, 146, 265
Telephone Dialing 259
Tianguis...73, 136, 165, 166, 167, 182
Time Zone 21
Tinaco...*See* Water:Tank (Tinaco)
Tipping...24, 88, 100, 140, 141, 145, 153, 175, 213
Tlaquepaque 148, 180
Toll Toads (cuotas) 96

Tonalá..........................148, 180
Tour Packages......................20
Tours.............20, 148, 180, 241
TV...55, 81, 86, 103, 219, 223, 224, 226, 242
USPS Airmail M-Class ..57, 74
Utilities................102, 103, 214
Vehicles
   Accident Form................290
   Accidents...69, 94, 97, 112, 121, 153, 154, 155, 193, 195, 270, 276, 280, 281, 283, 285, 286, 288, 290
   Brokers...........................161
   Buying and Selling.........159
   Cost of.........................50, 51
   Deposit................89, 92, 239
   Foreign-Plated...51, 160, 161, 162, 237, 240
   Impounding...112, 121, 155, 161, 162, 269, 270, 271, 276
   License Plates...51, 151, 152, 153, 158, 159, 160, 269, 270, 272, 273, 276
   Nationalizing...................159
   Permit...38, 50, 90, 91, 92, 93, 94, 110, 114, 115, 116, 151, 152, 162, 237

Registration Plates..........151
Repair..............................156
Smog Sticker...................153
Stolen.............................160
Visas............................236, 265
   FM-2...40, 66, 110, 115, 152, 160, 197, 232, 237, 239, 240, 241, 242, 243, 247
   FM-3...19, 39, 40, 66, 80, 110, 114, 115, 116, 152, 162, 197, 232, 233, 237, 238, 239, 241, 242, 243, 247
   Working Permissions...39, 40, 177, 237
Water...78, 100, 101, 102, 104, 105, 168, 169, 170, 209, 214, 215, 216
   Cistern (Aljibe)........105, 215
   Disinfectants...................172
   Pressure...30, 104, 215, 216, 218
   Purification...30, 101, 172, 216, 218
   Tank (Tinaco) ..30, 104, 215
Weapons..........82, 96, 122, 188
Web Boards........................261

Made in the USA
Lexington, KY
04 May 2014